CHAPTER

11

FACING IT?
I did too.

Janet Chihocky

with Heather B. Hayes

CHAPTER 11
FACING IT?
I did too.

Copyright © 2020 Janet Chihocky
Published by 21st Century Press
Springfield, MO 65807

21st Century Press is a Christian publisher dedicated to publishing books that have a high standard of family values. We believe the vision for our books is to provide families and individuals with user-friendly materials that will help them in their daily lives and experiences. It is our prayer that this book will help you discover Biblical truth for your own life and help you meet the needs of others. May God richly bless you.

21st Century Press
2131 W. Republic Rd.
PMB 211
Springfield, MO 65807

Cover Design: Rachel Phillips
Photography: Clark Vandergrift
Book Design: Lee Fredrickson
ISBN   TBook: 978-1-951774-16-5
       eBook: 978-1-951774-17-2

Visit our website at: www.21stcenturypress.com
Printed in the United States of America

21stCENTURY
P R E S S
READING YOU LOUD AND CLEAR

DEDICATION

For everybody who believed in me—when there
wasn't a lot of reason to believe.

AUTHOR'S NOTE

The people in this book are real. I have used the actual names of many of the characters in my story, either because they are aware that I am including them and have given me permission to do so or because they are public figures and the events of their lives and careers are already part of the public record. However, I have also chosen to use pseudonyms for some characters to protect their privacy and guard their reputations. The purpose of writing this book was to tell my story, not to shine a bright, unanticipated spotlight on anyone's actions, whether those actions were unbelievably generous or less than noble. I am grateful to all of those people whose lives intersected with mine—in good ways and not so good—because God was able to bring everything together for His own purposes, which are sometimes mysterious but always greater and more impactful than we can ever imagine.

CONTENTS

1. A Gift Squandered 7

2. From Brokenness, Rage And Red Plastic Cups 25

3. We Are Go For Launch 43

4. Bad Faith, Good Faith 65

5. Starting Over, "Again" 83

6. Where is That FedEx Truck? 101

7. From Out of the Past 123

8. Business Matters 139

9. Fuel for the Journey 155

10. Breaking Out 169

11. Unexpected Deliverance 183

CHAPTER 11

— ONE —

A GIFT SQUANDERED

Though I walk in the midst of trouble, You will revive me. The Lord will perfect that which concerns me. Psalm 138:7-8

"Your business is spiraling out of control," the accountant stated bluntly. "You need to call a lawyer."

"For what?" I asked, puzzled. Had I underpaid my taxes? I thought. Not filled out the right paperwork?

He stared at me for a moment, and I continued to mentally reach about, clutching my way towards something plausible, something that made sense. I came up empty. I was truly in the dark, completely unaware that what I saw as the foundation of my day-to-day existence was about to drop out from under me like a sinkhole.

The meeting had been set up without much notice or explanation, but I wasn't concerned. I had started my company, JANSON, five years prior and had hired this particular accounting firm on the advice of my then banker. The CPAs there had since then been competent but dispassionate in their management of my cash flow projections and expenditures, and I was quite used to sitting through the necessary but tedious explanations of quarterly financial statements.

JANSON had literally been a dream come true for me: the opportunity to operate a small marketing and communications firm that specialized in meeting the unique needs of the aerospace industry. I was 28 years old at the time, energetic, sure of myself and ready to take on the world. I'd spent a decade working in the communications department at Orbital Sciences Corporation, a young company that had developed a breakthrough launch vehicle that sent satellites into low-Earth orbit—not from the ground but from an aircraft flying at an altitude of 40,000 feet.

I'd first gotten hired by chance while I was still in high school and made the most of it, going above and beyond everything that was expected of me, studying the ins and outs of the industry and making all the right connections. It was the 1990s, a heady time for anyone working in the Washington, D.C., National Capital Region.

Orbital encouraged everyone to think big, and I soon found myself thinking even bigger. I had always had an entrepreneurial spirit and I was itching to test my full potential. In the few months before I took the plunge, though, I prayed for discernment. Should I leave a job with great security and good pay to go out on my own? Was this God's will for me?

In time, I was convicted that the answer was a resounding "Yes!" In 1998, JANSON was founded. My confidence in the rightness of my decision soared when, out of the gate, we landed the advertising account of a prestigious aerospace giant on the west coast that had been a leading player in the global commercial satellite industry. It seemed so easy.

Nearly five years on, JANSON had enjoyed a lot of success. When people asked, I would assure them that my employees and I were doing quite well. JANSON had great clients. The company had ongoing work. I was seeking out new business, and I had set long-term goals. My golf game was improving. What could be wrong?

My optimism, though, belied the operational, financial and cultural cavities that for some time had been silently forming under the company's carefully constructed underpinnings. My focus was always on sales, client deliverables and client relations, not operations, and I didn't have wise financial counsel telling me what to do—and, more importantly, what not to do. I was flying high, but I didn't have someone in the co-pilot's seat helping me to accurately read the instrumentation and stay on course if heavy fog ever began to cloud my view.

At the same time, there were larger forces that were putting downward pressure on all businesses. As I climbed into my sporty red Honda Accord on that cold day in February, the entire country was in a state of extreme uncertainty. We were not quite six months beyond the September 11 terrorist attacks on the World Trade Center towers and the Pentagon, located just miles away. The U.S. had already invaded Afghanistan and toppled the Taliban regime, which had provided a safe harbor for the al-Qaeda terror group and its masterminds.

A lot of companies were bearing the brunt of this "new normal." More than 18,000 small businesses had failed or would soon fail or be displaced.[1] The aerospace industry, largely because of massive losses to the airlines, took an economic hit in the billions of dollars. And as is typical in an economic downturn, a lot of companies had put the brakes on their advertising and marketing spend.

---

[1] "The Economic Effects of 9/11: A Retrospective Assessment," Report to Congress, Gail Makinen, Coordinator Specialist in Economic Policy Government and Finance Division, Congressional Research Office, Sept. 27, 2002.

At JANSON, though, we were holding our own, or so I thought. We had a couple of large "anchor" clients, along with some relatively new clients, and we were working hard on rebranding projects for two of them. Among other things, we were creating new logos, new websites and new marketing materials. Sure, sales had slowed quite a bit due to the economic environment and we'd taken on debt to sustain the operations. But wasn't that what every business did from time to time to get through the tough times?

As I weaved my way through traffic on that Friday afternoon, though, I wasn't thinking too much about work. I was already in weekend mode, dressed casually in a sweater and black jeans and ready to get started catching up on errands, spending time with my family and then on Sunday enjoying a full day of church activities and socializing.

When I arrived, a secretary led me into the senior accountant's office, and he stood, unsmiling, behind the desk to greet me. He was wearing dark gray pants, a crisp white shirt and colorful suspenders, clothes that were hardly in keeping with the earth-shattering news that he was about to tell me.

After some small talk and his initial statement telling me that I needed to hire an attorney, I pulled myself together, valiantly putting on my executive face and manner: I raised my chin, looked him in the eye and asked pointedly, "Why would I need to call a lawyer?"

"You need to consider filing for Chapter 11," he stated matter-of-factly.

Wait a minute—what? Hesitating, I carefully asked him to clarify. "Are you saying that I need to file for bankruptcy?"

I watch his face twist up, and I could tell he was trying to speak as precisely as possible. "I am advising you to take the weekend to prepare and then to call a lawyer on Monday," he stated, punching out each word as if he was worried I still might not get what he was trying to say.

He didn't say that I *had* to file, but perhaps professional ethics didn't allow him to be so candid. The implication, though, was clear: He and his partners didn't think JANSON could survive and I needed to act quickly to get ahead of the crisis.

I breathed out quietly, so he didn't sense my distress. Within, though, I was gasping: What? Are you kidding me? What are you *talking* about?

Probably anticipating my disbelief, the accountant picked up my thick file and gestured to indicate that he held the damning evidence needed to convict me fully. "Janet, we have looked at the numbers, run the numbers over and over, and we just cannot see how you are going to get out of this."

He then flipped back to the first page and started reciting hard truths about the hot mess my finances were in. I tried to listen, but the words faded out as my own thoughts took over and began to translate. The people I had paid to advise me were telling me that my company had no future. How could I not know things were this bad? And now there was no hope?

It was at that point that I realized that I had failed and not just financially. I had failed at business. I had allowed this billowing jumble of debt and mismanagement to grow out of control. JANSON needed a strong fiscal manager, someone who could hold expenses down, make the hard cuts when they needed to happen. It needed someone who could have anticipated and prepared for the hard times.

I hadn't been that person. I had networked, made the sales,

brought on the clients, hired the employees, led the projects, worked to keep everyone happy. I had focused on all the things I was great at, the things that I enjoyed doing. But the financial management, the strategic planning, the HR issues, the fundamentals of solid business operation—those were outside my comfort zone and so I didn't spend a lot of time on them. Instead, I outsourced the basics to an outside firm without truly understanding what I needed them to do to help the business successfully navigate the ups and downs of the business cycle.

The business books had been right. Starting the company had been the easiest part. Keeping it going, that was really hard. I was like the novice skier who headed straight to the black diamond slopes, more focused on the potential thrills than the dangers. I was like the would-be parent who focuses more on the excitement of decorating a nursery or the comfort of holding a happy, cooing baby than on the heart-wrenching possibilities that might come along farther down the road, like colic, developmental delays, school bullying and teenage rebellion.

A big, red failure button started to blink inside my head. I was the leader of my company and I hadn't prepared myself and those in my sphere for any of the uncomfortable and dangerous scenarios that might lie ahead. I felt embarrassed, of course, but my shame was soon fueled by a more disturbing reality. God had gifted this business to me, and I had blown it.

Pride goeth before destruction. Had I been prideful? Maybe not in the typical way, but once I had gotten the business underway, I had leaned too often on my own understanding. I had assumed that my strengths—my gift for marketing, my knack for managing relationships, my deep understanding of industry dynamics, my ability to make a sale and close a deal—were enough to ensure ongoing success. But I had never taken an honest assessment of my weaknesses. If I had, I might have realized that I needed to work a lot harder to acquire other, equally critical skills. Maybe I should have spent nights and weekends getting an executive MBA. Maybe I should have pursued more on-the-job operational and management experience before making the move to start my own company.

But I hadn't. I had felt called to start the business, but once it was underway, I had treated it at times like a jaunt, like I was out for a cruise on the Love Boat, only to suddenly find that I'd booked passage on the Titanic. And now, here I was, plunging straight to the bottom.

I had taken advantage of God's gift, and now this expert was confirming to me that there was no way to go back and do it differently, to do it right. The accountant dropped the file back down on his desk, startling me back to the present.

"So, give it some thought this weekend. I really encourage you to find a lawyer and then get back to me on Monday, so we can help start the process," he instructed.

I stood up and nodded, ignoring his outstretched hand even as I lurched toward the door and then accelerated out of his office and towards the parking lot in a vain effort to check my emotions. I lost the battle and began crying just as I climbed back into my car. I wondered if I could even drive out of the parking lot, much less make it all the way home. My emotions defied description. I imagined myself standing at the edge of a cliff looking straight down into nothingness. I was numb, afraid, lost, alone. The gray sky overhead was growing darker and more threatening, adding to the sense of cold despair that threatened to overtake me. I made it onto the main road before my sobs became so overwhelming that I had to pull over.

I cried and cried, and I kept on crying. How could this be?

Bankruptcy? When I woke up this morning, I had a business that was operating as usual and now it was in jeopardy. To file for bankruptcy was to bring finality. Was this really the end of all that I had worked for? And what did "the end" mean? Was my career over? What would I do? What would happen to my employees? Would my freelancers and vendors get paid for work they'd already done? Was everything I knew going to be over and done?

Prayers and pleas were forming in my mind even as I pulled out my cell phone and considered calling the people who could provide the most comfort—and the best advice for how I was going to cope with the humiliation, the stinging rebuke, the irrevocability of a Chapter 11 bankruptcy filing.

But who to call? I was afraid to voice my embarrassment and afraid of getting the wrong advice. I was vulnerable, and I knew it. How would I react if someone responded, "Go ahead and file"? What if they made it easy for me to justify the decision with platitudes like "A lot of people have done it" or "It's not the worst thing that could happen"? Did I only want someone to tell me what I wanted to hear? Would I be open to hard truths? Would someone have the guts to tell me what I needed to hear? I started driving again and asked God to show me who I should contact at this moment. I needed the right counsel.

I pulled over again, reaching into my purse to search for some tissue. After wiping my eyes and face and getting my emotions back under control, I finally felt ready to listen. I started making phone calls. The first one was to an industry friend from my days at Orbital. Karen was then a program manager at Hercules Aerospace and one of the brightest people I knew. She had what I describe as superior management skills, superior business instincts. When I blubbered out my devastating news, I was taken aback to learn that Karen wasn't immediately resigned to defeat as the accountants had been. And she didn't think I should be resigned to it either.

"Janet," she said, "when times are good, your business is demonstrating that it is committed to you. However, when times are difficult, that is when you show that you are committed to your business. You're a strong person, Janet. Explore all of your options before you consider calling a lawyer."

I listened carefully, encouraged. It was fantastic business advice, probably the best I've ever heard, before or since. Even now, I find myself translating that message into practical and spiritual terms. How easy is it to be committed to a marriage when you're still in the honeymoon phase? How easy is it to be a parent when your child is affectionate, healthy and well-behaved? How easy is it to be committed to God, to have faith, when everything is going our way and life is picture-perfect? How often do we question our faith and lose all hope when things go awry, when we lose something dear, be it a business or our health or a loved one? I had faith—but had it ever really been challenged?

Soon I called my mother. She hadn't initially been enthusiastic about my decision to start my own company; in fact, she had begged me not to trade in the security of a good-paying, salaried position at Orbital for the risky existence of an entrepreneur. Given that, I was expecting something on the order of "I told you so." But she surprised me.

Now, when it looked like gainful employment might have actually been the right path for me all along, my mother was suddenly advocating for the road less traveled. "Jan, I know this is hard, but God will show you what to do." She said it firmly, without any doubt in her voice.

A s I hung up the phone, I pondered what I felt like God was telling me: Janet, it's a difficult season, but will you stay committed to me? Will you trust me?

Clearly, I was being tested. How much did my business really mean to me? Was I going to abandon it now that it was on life support and the going was going to get really tough and really uncertain? If I rejected the accountant's advice, I would need God's guidance to figure out what to do, but was I wise enough as a child of God to truly know what His voice sounded like? I thought I did, but I wasn't completely sure. And that scared me.

The truth was, I really didn't want to want to file for Chapter 11. At least not without a fight. I was afraid of being labeled a failure, but I also wanted to try and keep running JANSON long enough for its debts to be paid off. I might have to close the books on JANSON but I didn't want to close the books on my freelancers and the small vendors and the creditors until I'd settled up all the accounts. They hadn't done anything wrong and they needed the money. For some of my smallest consultants, an unpaid invoice could hurt their ability to pay a mortgage or health insurance premium. The larger creditors could write it off, but I still didn't want JANSON's legacy to be sullied for all time as a deadbeat, a once-thriving company that had helped itself but left others high and dry.

"Owe no man." I knew Romans 13:8 intimately, having sat through many a sermon about Biblical finances. Was it a sin to file for bankruptcy? Maybe, if the action was taken flippantly, without regard for others, without trying as hard as you could to put things right. As I pondered my situation, I knew I wouldn't feel right walking away from the people I owed money to and I definitely wanted to try to pay them back, even if it took five years. After I did that, maybe then, I would be right to close up the business and return to a safe, salaried position with a stable employer.

I pulled into my garage and put the gear into park, still deep in my head. I wanted to trust that God could take this horrible situation I had created and somehow make it work for His larger purpose. But what do you do when you cannot see a way out and when you feel like a complete failure? I sincerely questioned if I had enough faith in myself and enough faith in God to reject the accountant's advice.

Fear and doubt again took over as I opened the door to my townhouse and slumped into my favorite chair. It felt like heavy weights were shackled to my hands, feet and neck, and I could feel my body and soul moan silently at the burden of it. From what the accountant had said, JANSON owed a mountain of debt that I would have to tackle. How could I do that? I had failed the business when I was starting with a clean balance sheet. What made me think I could do better when everything was stacked against me?

My emotions were back in full swing. I cried and I prayed. I put on a CD by Sandi Patty, the most popular Christian artist at the time, and played it over and over. *"There've been dreams I forgot and dreams I let die, unnoticed sunsets in front of my eyes,"* she sang sweetly as if she knew my story. *"I just couldn't see them. I thought I didn't need them."*

I blubbered along. *"Sure there are things I'd do differently, and yet Your grace gives me days where I simply forget.... You set me free from my befores and afters, from a debt I know I'll never pay...."*

After some time, I finally climbed into bed and said: "Lord, I am so sorry that I took for granted this gift you gave me, that I abused it."

I fell into a fitful sleep but woke up suddenly at 4 a.m. Still, I could feel the heaviness of the previous day's events on me. I could feel myself descending into a pit of despair as I contemplated my choice: file for bankruptcy or somehow try to save my fast-sinking business.

I began to pray. "Lord, I know you're trying to speak to me right now, but I need you to make this really black and white because I don't know if I have it in me for anything that's gray."

And then I heard a voice, clear, commanding, calm. "I am not a God of bankruptcy."

Was that it? Was that my answer? I knew others who had filed for bankruptcy, and I certainly didn't judge them for it. It might have been the right journey for them, but was it God's chosen path for me? In my case, maybe His purposes would be fulfilled in my at least trying to hang onto my business.

At 6 a.m. I picked up the phone to call Jeanette, a longtime friend. Jeanette is 25 years older than me, and I first met her when I was a 12th grade student taking her Spanish class. She is also one of the most God-filled people I've ever known, with a faith that is both genuine and deep. This faith didn't falter through the most difficult chapters of her life, including a battle with breast cancer.

I have found through the years that God can bring people into your life who will stretch you in your faith, who encourage you to keep raising the bar. Despite our age difference and initial teacher-student dynamic, Jeanette and I became good friends over the years. She was a mentor of sorts, but it wasn't the type of official arrangement where we met once a week for a structured meeting where she taught and I learned. Instead, I absorbed her lessons and advice through deep conversations about our daily lives and lots and lots and lots of prayer.

Jeanette seemed to have been waiting for my call that Saturday morning because she didn't pick up the phone with a "Hello?" Instead, she answered, "Jan, the Lord has had you on my heart."

Just hearing her voice about did me in, and I must have sounded devastated to her, truly at rock bottom. I shared all of my pain and fear as I recounted the details of the previous day. She did her best to console me, citing comforting Bible verses and reminding me of God's compassionate nature and His truths.

I felt myself regaining my emotional footing and wiped my eyes, cleared my throat and told her the dilemma that I was facing: "Jeanette, I don't know how He's going to do it, but I believe God's telling me not to close this business."

Jeanette didn't hesitate. "Jan, I feel the same, so we're going to pray, and we're going to pray right now for God to continue to reveal Himself to you every minute of every day."

And so we did. We thanked God for all of His provision. We asked Him to provide strength and wisdom for this journey.

When we finished, I felt even more certain that God wanted me to keep going with JANSON, but I still was fearful because I did not know when or where the "deliverance" would come from. Perhaps there's a reason that the phrase "do not be afraid," or some similar take on it, is listed over 200 times in the Bible.

I spent the entire Saturday contacting family and friends. "I do not think that I am to close this business, but I need people praying," I told them.

I went to the morning worship service on Sunday at the local Baptist church, where I was very active, but made it a point to sit in the back, largely out of view. I felt emotionally drained and, despite my best efforts to hide it, my face was still puffy and splotchy. As the music for the opening song started, I began to tear up. People couldn't help but notice. Just because you know that God has led you to a decision doesn't necessarily mean that the journey or the "burden" of the journey instantly switches from a rocky road to a smooth road. I was about to embark on a faith walk like never before, and I was afraid. My friend Jeanne later told me that I looked absolutely lost. And that's exactly how I felt: lost. There was no roadmap forward, just a vast, seemingly endless wilderness with no signposts.

After the service and unknown to me, Jeanne met with the pastor. She shared my dilemma and asked if the church leadership could encourage me with prayer. I was in my car, ready to go home when Jeanne came outside and asked me to please come back that night. So I did. After the evening service, Jeanne, the pastor and several deacons formed a circle around me and laid their hands on my shoulders. Each of them took turns praying for me.

Then the pastor, a gifted vocalist, began singing one of his favorite hymns: "Have Thine Own Way, Lord."

Have Thine own way, Lord! Have Thine own way!
Thou art the Potter, I am the clay.
Mold me and make me after Thy will,
While I am waiting, yielded and still.

The hymn had been written by Adelaide Pollard, a 40-year-old Bible teacher who desperately wanted to go to Africa on a mission trip but could not raise enough funds for the journey. Discouraged and uncertain about her future, she decided to attend an evening prayer service, where she overheard an elderly woman talking to God: "It doesn't matter what You bring into our lives, Lord," the woman quietly prayed. "Just have Your own way with us." Pollard was so inspired that she went home and wrote a four-stanza poem in one sitting. The song was later set to music and has been a go-to staple in the Baptist hymnal ever since.

The singing reached a crescendo as the pastor and deacons moved into the last stanza:

Have Thine own way, Lord! Have Thine own way!
Hold o'er my being absolute sway!
Fill with Thy Spirit 'till all shall see
Christ only, always, living in me.

I closed my eyes and carefully took in each word. This was a hymn I'd known and sung in church and Sunday school since I was a child, but I had never heard it quite like this. It suddenly meant something very clear, very real. I needed to admit my soul's desire to have God truly in charge, to turn everything over to Him, and that wasn't an easy step for a naturally born controlling person.

"Have thine own way, Lord," I whispered. I was making a declaration, finally allowing myself to really let go and let God take over. "Your way, God, not mine."

I was walking through a dark place, but I wasn't alone. The God of this universe who cared about me more than I could imagine would give me exactly what I needed, exactly when I needed it. I was 32 years old and single, but God promised that He would be more than just my Savior. He would become my closest friend. He just needed me to keep turning it over to Him, to be faithful and to give up the guilt. The submission and the faithfulness would get easier, but the giving up of the guilt—that would take a long time.

As the pastor's melodic voice punctuated each word of the final line, I felt a powerful peace and sureness wash over me. No matter what the balance sheet said, no matter the size of the debt or how impossible it seemed, I would not file for bankruptcy. God had His reasons. They were meant for good, and I was going to trust Him with everything I had.

The next morning, I called my accountant's office. The senior partner was on the phone, along with others, waiting to hear which lawyer I would contact so they could start the complicated process that lay ahead. They were pragmatic and detached, completely certain that their hard calculations laid out the only way forward for my company and me.

They knew numbers and they knew my business, but they didn't know what they didn't know. Maybe they had an inkling of what God could do, or maybe they didn't know. Either way, their expensive advice was no longer of concern to me. So, I got right to the point. "These doors are not closing," I stated. "At least not until I pay off the people I owe."

I ignored the silence on the other end of the phone. It lasted for what felt like a long time, and I wondered if they would surprise me and get on board with my plan. It wasn't the easy way to go, but I was sure it was going to be worth the effort. Before long, though, I heard some muffled mumbling and paper being shuffled off the desk. The senior accountant cleared his throat. "If that's your decision, we'll have to cease our relationship with you immediately," he said.

"Of course," I replied. The accountant didn't expect me to make it and I didn't care.

It wasn't that I needed them to agree with me or tell me what I wanted to hear. I had always been open to being challenged, to debating. I liked hearing different ideas and different perspectives. Getting the right inputs, however uncomfortable, is critical to making good, informed decisions, both in business and in life. I understood that and welcomed it. But this wasn't healthy pushback on the part of the accountants—this was acquiescence, defeat. I was their client, and they didn't care about me or about achieving the outcomes I believed were important to pursue.

My future was now in God's hands, and I made a silent vow that never again would I work with anyone who didn't believe in me—especially when I was trying to do the right thing.

I was ready to step out in faith. Even though God had given me clarity on which door to walk through, I had no idea what the coming days, weeks or months would look like. All I knew was that He would be with me.

CHAPTER 11

TWO

FROM BROKENNESS, RAGE AND RED PLASTIC CUPS

Therefore, do not be unwise, but understand what the will of the Lord is. Ephesians 5:17

A s I sat down at my desk after hanging up the phone with the accountant, I took a deep breath and let out an even deeper sigh as I realized that the decision to keep JANSON open was only the first—and likely the easiest step—in my journey.

I looked at the action box sitting on my desk and the project files that were piled up nearby and then glanced outside. In the bleak light of another cold winter morning, I felt my earlier zeal begin to wane and I slumped forward, putting my hands in my lap and staring at my fingers. *How in the world was I going to do this?* I suddenly felt broken. I was like the wife who had tried everything to hold her husband's loyalty, only to watch him walk out the door, or the associate who had worked for years to get the partnership, only to get passed over in favor of someone else. What was I thinking? Did I really have what it took to keep going, to hang on and find a way to pay off all my debtors?

There were no rose-colored glasses big enough to hide the

reality of what I was facing. This was not going to be easy. Though I hadn't yet tallied the exact numbers, I knew that JANSON was in extreme debt for a firm of its size. We had ongoing work, but not nearly enough. We had way too much overhead. And creditors would soon start phoning, demanding payment.

I turned on the computer, and as I waited for it to boot up, I could see my reflection in the screen. My eyes were still puffy, my shoulders and upper back were bent down like something had fallen directly on my head. I really was broken, I thought. And weren't broken things useless, unable to perform even their basic function, no matter what they were originally built for?

I shook my head and tried to recall my strong certainty of the evening prior. God loved all of us no matter what. He could take broken pieces and not only put it all back together but make it into something entirely new, something better, something stronger. That was what His grace was all about. That was what the Cross was all about.

God had a plan for me, I reminded myself, and it wouldn't come to fruition if I didn't somehow stay in the game. Clicking on my email program, I started browsing through the myriad entries that had come through overnight. Maybe there was a client letting me know of their pressing need to get a major project underway right away. I kept looking but nothing jumped out. If God had a way forward, I didn't see it, and I could feel my frustration already starting to build.

Instinctively, I wanted to rush in and force things to happen—and happen quickly. However, I knew that God's plan would inevitably require me to wait. This was going to be extremely hard for me. I am not a naturally patient person; actually, I could be a real hothead. Left to my own devices, I would race forward like one of the bulls of Pamplona, charging over anything that got in my way, but ultimately ending up in a place of destruction, not victory.

Taking God's more deliberate plan for my life required me to plant a seed of trust, to pray and then to wait—and likely wait some more. I would need to have the understanding that, in His good time, not mine, it would work out and work out better than I could ever envision. I had seen this before through different difficulties and different crises, but no matter how well I thought I understood this process, I often fought against it.

In hindsight, though, I could clearly see where God had made the difference. Things had always seemed to somehow turn out for the better, over and over again in both my personal life and my career when I had been more willing to trust that God would sort it all out.

So, as I stared at my computer, I tried again to surrender it all to God: my angst, my brokenness, the work, the future. He could handle what I couldn't, and I had to find a way to also listen for God's guidance as to what "my part" would be. Despite the amazing events of the weekend, I still doubted whether I could really recognize His voice in the din of daily life.

I bowed my head and prayed for strength and faith. Then I grabbed a pad of paper and a pen and started to think through my day. Without a doubt, the first thing I needed to do was to call together my small staff and let them know what was happening. The company was in trouble, but they needed to know that I was not filing for Chapter 11. They all knew I was a Christian, so they wouldn't be surprised when I told them that I believed God was going to turn it all around, that I felt led to keep going. But my words wouldn't be enough. They wouldn't believe me or follow me into the breach unless my faith shined through in both my attitude and my actions.

Buying time and trying to motivate myself, I anxiously tapped my pencil a few times, jotted down some notes and then looked around my office, realizing for the first time how void it was of any profound quotes on the secrets of great leadership. The leased suite, made up of my office and two others plus a lobby and administrative area, wasn't terribly fancy. I had chosen it because it was affordable. In fact, the price was so right that the previous summer, in anticipation of hiring more employees and growing our productivity, I'd leased another 1,000 square feet of office space just across the hall. As the economy sank over the last few months of 2001, though, we never went any further, so now it just sat there empty, serving to only help grow our negative cash flow.

I got up, opened the door to my office and looked out into the lobby area where my mom sat at her desk. For some time now, she had worked as JANSON's receptionist. It wasn't just that she needed the job; she was really quite good at it, always at the ready to welcome visitors or answer the phone cheerfully. Most of the time clients and industry partners would call just to chitchat with Mom! I smiled as I reflected on her flamboyant style and untiring spirit. She too had been through her fair share of challenges, but no matter how difficult, she somehow managed to hold onto a deeply held conviction that God would take care of everything in His time, in His way.

For as long as I could remember, Mom believed that all of life's bumps were an opportunity to build character and draw closer to God. She faced everything with a spirit of determination and faith, and she encouraged me to do the same. Mom would never let one of us kids sit around and wallow in pity or whine too much about the unfairness of some problem or conflict we were dealing with.

"Brace up," she'd demand, raising her chin resolutely and somehow mixing her stern tone with just the right amount of empathy and compassion. "Life will either make you or it will break you."

At the same time, her faith is what gave her the power to persevere during hard times, a state that proved a near-constant companion for much of her adult life. A vivid memory from my early childhood was walking into the kitchen early in the morning to see my mother drinking a cup of black coffee and reading her Bible.

In these quiet times, Mom was simply and steadily adding to the foundation of trust and resilience that she had gained while growing up as one of only two girls in a rural family of 13 children. Her father, Lester Bolton, was the sheriff of Anderson County, Tennessee, a mountainous region that once played a role in the Manhattan Project and the development of the first atomic bomb. Her mother, Stella Mae, maintained law and order on the home front, successfully transforming the couple's noisy, overwhelming family life into a haven of affection, faith and loyalty.

My mother regularly describes her childhood as not merely happy but completely joyous. Her siblings were her playmates and confidantes, and they would all remain close—and available to each other—for their entire lives.

Mom was naturally exuberant, active and confident, traits that would serve her well when she and a couple of girlfriends decided to move to the Washington, D.C., area in search of better job opportunities than they could find in eastern Tennessee. She was tapped to be a secretary at the Pentagon during the early Eisenhower administration and soon met my father, Gilbert, who was serving in the Army. They got married and lived the nomadic life of a military couple, moving every so often as Dad took on assignments in New York, Georgia, Texas, Germany and other locales. After nine years, they welcomed their first child, my brother, and then, three years later, in 1967, my sister. I arrived in 1970.

By then, my father had retired from the Army and started working a myriad of different jobs, some of which were exceptionally well-paying. He and Mom bought a large, beautiful home in a well-to-do neighborhood in northern Virginia and complemented it with an in-ground swimming pool, outdoor playhouses and a tire swing for us kids. Mom, following her own mother's example, took us regularly to church.

That happy picture soon faded. I was just six years old when my mother informed my siblings and me that our Dad had left and that we were moving. I was too young to understand fully why my parents were getting a divorce, and I don't remember much about that time. All I know is that I was, first and foremost, a Mama's girl, and as long as I was with my mother, I was content. I can only imagine how hard it must have been for her, but Mom bravely picked up the pieces, bid goodbye to our upscale home in the suburbs and moved us into a small apartment in a nearby town.

I grew up attending a large Baptist church in Fairfax, Virginia, and, like my siblings before me, was enrolled in the affiliated Christian school, starting in kindergarten. After my parents divorced, my mom felt that it was critical for all of us kids to continue to have a strong, Christ-focused education, though the tuition was beyond her means.

To make ends meet, she worked a full-time administrative

job at the school, in addition to driving a school bus. Somehow, through the grace of God and the occasional miraculous gift that seemed to come out of nowhere at the moment when it was needed most, Mom would overcome all kinds of challenges, financial and otherwise, and we all remained enrolled in the school through graduation.

The church and the school, all housed together on the same campus, became the core of my childhood. It was the source of most of my friends and most of my year-round activities, be it sports, youth group or revival services.

In time, my mother met a man at church and remarried. Her new husband had six of his own children from a prior marriage, and bringing the two families together further redefined our sense of normal as we all had to make adjustments and deal with what were sometimes chaotic moments and challenging situations.

Fortunately, as the youngest of all of the children, I was blessed with a highly social, fun-loving and adaptive personality. I was always keen to hang out with anyone, be they adults or neighborhood kids, and among my age group, I was the little ringleader, always taking the initiative to get my friends together to ride bikes, build forts, attend Bible school or play a game of kickball. At the same time, I was happy to stay in my room and creatively entertain myself, whether it was playing with toys or talking to my stuffed animals.

I also had a budding entrepreneurial spirit. In fact, even then, my sister made it a point to tell my mother that I seemed to have a real gift for closing deals. When I was just nine years old, I started selling custom Christmas cards for a national organization that enticed young people to hawk their products by giving out high-dollar prizes to top earners. In their brochure, I saw a boom box that I just had to have, so I took to the streets in my suburban neighborhood, selling door to door after school and hitting up some of the older ladies at church on Sunday.

"But Janet, it's not even autumn yet," one elderly neighbor gently pointed out when I showed up at her door one hot afternoon with a stack of sample cards bearing snow and Nativity scenes.

"Yes, but Christmas will be here before you know it, Mrs. Turner," I countered even as I started showing her some of her options. "This will be one less thing you'll have to worry about."

I did so well that not only did I earn that coveted boom box, but I won a gang of other prizes as well. I continued selling custom Christmas cards for another three years and always finished high on the list of top salespeople.

It helped that we were blessed with kind, friendly neighbors, and the Steins, a couple living right next door, happened to be the best of the lot. All of us kids liked to hang out at their house. They had a pool and offered us a standing invitation to come swim whenever we wanted, a highly generous offer that included any friends that we wanted to bring along. They even let us throw pool parties, so long as we promised to check and maintain the chlorine levels.

One night, we sent out a verbal invitation to a few select friends, and before long 30 to 40 church teens showed up. I dove into the middle of all that fun, happy to be hanging out with the "big kids." It nearly turned tragic, though. Some of the kids got bored and started shooting off bottle rockets. I was standing in the yard behind the pool when one screaming rocket went wildly off course and whizzed directly at me, smacking me just below my neck and leaving a blackened impact mark on my skin. Fortunately, it wasn't bad enough for me to need medical attention, but for sure, I felt like I'd been shot!

The pool parties continued, and we always had a great time, but to me, the Steins were like extended family. I hibernated in their home frequently, and I always wanted to go places with them, even if it was just to tag along on a bunch of errands on a Saturday afternoon.

I remember one evening lounging in their pool, looking up at the sky and suddenly declaring to no one in particular: "I'm going to own my own business one day." To my mind, a 1950s diner sounded perfect, a place where people could come and eat great food, dance to great music and have fun and be happy. I was just a kid dreaming out loud, but not in a million years could I have planned how it would ultimately turn out.

By the time I was a teenager, school and church activities began to dominate my daily schedule, and life took on a slightly more serious mood. At 14, while attending a revival service at my church, I officially accepted Christ as my Lord and Savior. Initially, it had seemed like any other day in church. I was sitting in a back pew, passing notes to my friends and being silly. But something in the sermon caught my attention, and I began listening intently. When one of the notes came back to me, I grabbed it without taking my eyes off of the pastor and put it away. I had been raised in the church, but suddenly I realized that I really couldn't be sure that Heaven would be my eternal dwelling place. As soon as the invitation went out for a chance to repent and choose a personal relationship with Jesus, I hurried down the aisle to answer the call. The pastor's wife lovingly greeted me and then smiled when I told her: "I want to be saved. I want to know for sure that Heaven will be my home one day." She put an arm around me, asked me to bow my head and prayed with me.

By then, I was just entering high school, and the lessons I would learn during that time played a huge role in my later career. The truth was, I was an average student, but I worked hard and excelled in certain areas, especially when inspired by a great teacher. Dr. David Reynolds, an English teacher and the public speaking coach, was one of my favorites. He convinced me to try out for a slot to represent the school in a public speaking competition.

To get on the team, I had to beat out a top contender named Billy, who was smart and very confident. I remember thinking, *There is NO way I can beat Billy*, but I did, and then I went on to win the school competition. Later that year, I was awarded first place in both the regional and state competitions for the Christian school association we were part of.

Once I got on the speaking kick, I absolutely loved it! And I still do to this day. It wasn't just being on stage that hooked me but making the delivery, connecting with the story, persuading the audience. My speeches were usually declarative and about topics that I felt passionate about. They ran the gamut, but often they touched on politics and patriotism. One of my favorite speeches was titled, "I Am the American Flag."

If I was inspired, I could also inspire the audience, Dr. Reynolds would insist. And he, in turn, inspired me. He was upbeat, always encouraging me to speak with conviction, to speak clearly and to never set limits on myself. "You can do this, Janet," he would chatter excitedly during my practice sessions. "You can get a big win. Matter of fact, I can see you running for president one day!"

Over the next four years, I won four regional and three state championships for declarative speaking. I was honored to represent the school, but I was—and still am—highly competitive. It wasn't enough for me just to participate. I wanted to win! And if I lost, I pushed myself that much harder, so I could be better the next time and, hopefully, take the top spot. Very often, that's exactly what would happen. And that made it all the more enjoyable because I absolutely loved carrying home those first-place trophies.

My high school years were some of the best of my life, but the school itself had the legalistic, fundamentalist philosophy that permeated the Baptist culture in the 1980s. The emphasis was on performance, on works, on following the "law" to the letter, and that left very little room for grace. As a young Christian, the culture gave me a distorted view of what being a Christ-follower was really all about. The truth is that, no matter what our individual merits, none of us can work hard enough or perform well enough to get to Heaven, but Jesus loved us enough to provide us a way. He paid the price for our weaknesses, our infirmities, our brokenness on the Cross. It was through His brokenness and His death and His resurrection that He offers—and we can receive—the gifts of forgiveness, second chances, grace and, ultimately, eternal life.

Unfortunately, that's not what I and other students were learning at this school. They harped a little too much on the law, pushing the gift of grace far into the background, and they expected all of us students to walk a very straight line. Those who did were rewarded with praise and a sense that they were somehow superior, while those who didn't, those who stumbled or, worse, purposefully stepped off that line in a moment of teenage impulse or rebellion, were met with not just harsh consequences but harsh judgment. Whether it was intended or not, the distorted lesson was clear to those who didn't perform like they should: Some Christians were "better" than others, and that drove a lot of students to doubt Christ's perfect love or, worse, walk away from Him.

In the 11th grade, I came face to face with the destructive nature of this legalistic philosophy, and it soon led to my first major fight with my mother. The conflict came when I informed her that I wanted to leave the school. She had made so many sacrifices for so many years to give my siblings and I the best possible education, but I didn't care. I just wanted out.

At the time, I was playing basketball, my other major extracurricular activity. I loved the game and, as with my public speaking, I was extremely competitive. I wasn't the highest scorer on the team, but I could play in the "paint" and I hustled on defense. Our coach that year was a kind man, confident, competitive and encouraging, infusing us with an overwhelming sense of optimism in our abilities and our prospects for the coming season.

That all changed one night when, after a basketball game, a group of players planned a victory party at a local Pizza Hut. I asked my mother if I could go and she agreed. I arrived at the party, which was fairly tame, and started hanging with my usual group of friends. The night sped by quickly and soon it was late. I knew I needed to get home but not before hanging out with another group of kids who were gathered on the far side of the parking lot and drinking out of red plastic cups. I wasn't naïve. I knew what they were doing. As I approached, I took a cup and tried to blend in. It was no big deal, right? What was the harm in trying it? I put the cup to my mouth and took a small sip, followed immediately by another sip. Ugh! I reactively spit out it out. I did *not* like the taste of beer. I wiped my mouth with the back of my hand, set the cup down and left, completely unconcerned about the fact that I was underage or that the school had a clear policy about alcohol use. I was instinctively more worried about missing my mom's curfew.

A couple of weeks later, I was called down to the school office. I suspected that something was up, but I didn't think I was in any kind of trouble—until I noticed that other students I had seen in the parking lot holding red plastic cups were also getting called down.

I knew I shouldn't have participated, but it was just a couple of sips. No big deal, right?

Wrong! It was a big deal. The principal and other staff who confronted me pulled out the rules of school engagement and pointed out the citation detailing that even a sip of alcohol was a violation. I sat, stunned, as I heard the principal begin to tick off my punishment:

"You are suspended from school for two weeks."

"You are off the basketball team."

"You will not represent the school this year in any competition for public speaking."

What?!! Are you kidding me? All this for taking a few sips and spitting it out? I was red-hot angry but also devastated. I went home and told my mom everything. "This is so wrong," I cried.

She agreed to take up my case before the school board to try to get the punishment overturned or at least lessened. She fought hard but got nowhere. The sentence stood. My two-week suspension began immediately, but it wasn't just some unexpected vacation. For every day I was out, I would get a zero in each class, which meant I'd have to attend summer school to make everything up and rescue my grades. Probably because she felt sorry for me and didn't want to leave me at home while she went to work, Mom allowed me to travel to Georgia during my suspension and visit my sister, who was attending college. I needed the break and I had a great time.

Still, I was livid over the decision. I felt like I and a few other students had been treated unfairly, and I wanted to run as far away as possible from that school and everyone in it. I just knew that the grass really would be greener at some other school—and that everyone would be a lot nicer and a lot more understanding. For the rest of the school year and into the summer break, especially when she carted me back and forth to summer school, I *begged* my mother to let me spend my final high school year somewhere else, anywhere else.

But Mom said no. And she held firm, no matter how many times I cried and pleaded. She agreed that the punishment wasn't right, but she also expected me to accept it, to brace up to it.

"Life is not always fair, Jan," Mom told me the first time I made my demand before lapsing into her usual platitude about how critical it was to use life's difficulties to "make" me, not break me.

There was a part of her that empathized with me, that felt for me, but she also believed deep in her soul that God wanted me at that school for some reason. She didn't understand why, but she believed without any doubt that this was His will for me and she obeyed.

"You're not leaving that school," she recited on numerous occasions. "You're going to finish your senior year there."

So, I unhappily headed back to school that fall, only to find that the one black mark on my record was still at the top of everyone's mind. "You'd better keep your nose clean," one teacher warned me. I had not lived right according to the law, and now I felt damned, marked as a troublemaker.

To make matters worse, I learned on my first day back that the girl's varsity team had a new basketball coach, Jim Rismiller, who was nothing like our old coach. I didn't think too highly of Coach Rismiller. As a former Air Force officer, he was loud and demanding. He was not very tall—most of us girls towered over him. He was always yelling at us during practice and games, and it irritated me. I didn't want to hear his mouth running, and I had a mouth on me that could match his, decibel for decibel. Arrogantly, I would fire back and challenge him. Not surprisingly, he picked someone else to be team captain, and that made me even more resentful.

Ironically, Coach Rismiller was married to Jeanette, my Spanish teacher, who I absolutely adored and who would later become my close friend and spiritual mentor. She was sweet and kind and compassionate. Jim? Not so much, or so I thought at the time. Perhaps if I'd had a better association with stable father figures, I might have noticed some of Jim's finer qualities, but I detested loud, controlling authority figures—and, in knee-jerk fashion, I determined that Coach Rismiller fit quite neatly in that category.

As the year progressed, I increasingly felt like I didn't belong, that I wasn't up to the school's standards. It didn't help when faculty announced that they would be naming a student as the "Most Likely to Succeed" based on the outcome of a special test and how well students had followed the rules during their high school career. Was someone's potential set by the age of 17? Was there no chance for redemption for any of us relative slackers?

Despite all my rage and insecurities, I pushed through that final year of school. I worked hard and did everything that I needed to finish strong, including winning first place in the state and regional competitions for public speaking and placing in the top five at nationals.

One mid-afternoon in early spring, I again walked into the office, this time to sign out for the day. As soon as I entered, the phone rang. The school secretary, Mrs. Mayhew, picked it up. "Good afternoon. How may I help you?" I heard her answer sweetly.

She continued the conversation, peppering moments of silence with the occasional "I see" and "uh-huh," but I was too busy flipping through pages in the logbook to try to figure out what they were talking about. Upon locating my name and making a notation in the time-out column, I started to head out the school door. As I passed by, Mrs. Mayhew abruptly held her hand up to stop me and then pulled the phone down to her shoulder, cupping the speaking end.

"Janet," she whispered. "A company is on the phone looking for a student to do part-time work. They are located just around the corner."

I asked her only one question: "How much are they paying?"

"$5.50 an hour."

"I'll take it!" I didn't care the name or the work. It was 1988, and as far as I was concerned, that was big money!

I drove over that afternoon, and when I walked into the lobby, I learned the name Orbital Sciences Corporation for the first time. On the wall was a stunning picture of a sleek rocket lifting off into space. I was in awe and couldn't wait to start.

In hindsight, I soon realized that while I had been damned by the law, God had given me grace. Because my mom had listened to His voice and challenged me to persevere and do the right thing, even in the face of injustice, I was where I was supposed to be. If my mother had let me run out on a tough situation, I never would have ended up with the up-and-coming aerospace giant that would launch me, out of the blue, into opportunities and destinations beyond my wildest imaginations.

And the basketball coach who could set my teeth to grinding would, years later, come back into my life in my darkest moments and help me find my way back towards a lighted path.

I was only just beginning to learn that what you initially see is often a long way from what you get—especially when God is in control.

CHAPTER 11

— THREE —

WE ARE GO FOR LAUNCH

Every valley shall be exalted and every mountain and hill brought low; the crooked places shall be made straight and the rough places smooth. Isaiah 40:4

JANSON had a small staff, so while I was everyone's boss, I also saw my full-time employees as friends and, in one instance, family. For this reason, I had already decided on that Monday morning to meet individually with each employee. I felt like it was important to give them the space and privacy they needed to freely discuss how JANSON's financial situation and my decision would affect their role in the company.

As I knocked on the door to the left of my office, I smiled to myself, feeling increasingly good about my decision to fight, to take a stand in defense of my company, to do everything I could to pay off the debt I owed. I didn't have much of a plan as yet, and I didn't have too many concrete answers to the likely questions the employees might ask about next steps, but we were a team, right? I was sure that everyone would share my determination to pull together and fight the battle that lay ahead, not unlike the way we would tackle a new client project.

We were all relatively young, energetic and self-confident. In the competitive world of marketing and advertising, we were an agile, innovative David. Time and again we had gone up against larger and well-established Goliaths to win the business and respect of prominent clients within the aerospace and defense markets. Our creative capabilities were strong—and I was sure that this innate talent would help us win over new clients, grow our revenue and pull us out of our current financial mire. We just needed to stick together and stick it out through this tough time.

The door opened and my creative director, Mike, casually waved me in. He seemed to stare right through me like he was deep in thought. It was a look I recognized as normal among my "right brain" types when they were on deadline, deep in their heads, unable to transition away from the focus required for concepting, designing, strategizing, creating. He moved back a couple of steps and sat down at his desk, where a large Apple monitor went silent as it transitioned to sleep mode.

"What's up?" he asked. Maybe it was my imagination, but as he took a sip of coffee and looked over the brim at me, he seemed guarded, even suspicious.

"Well, I just got off the phone with my accountant," I said, proceeding to provide cursory details of the meeting the previous Friday.

"I've decided not to file for bankruptcy," I stated. "I believe too much in this company. I've also come to believe that God doesn't want me to shut down and so I'm going to keep going."

He continued to stare at me but didn't respond, so I persisted in justifying my decision. "I am very optimistic, Mike. I really believe that we're going to get through this and JANSON could end up stronger than ever."

Mike looked away from me and then quickly dropped his attention to his desk, where he picked up some papers he'd been working from, straightened them and placed them into a folder.

"Janet, I appreciate your optimism," he said, "and I wish you the best of luck..." He paused long enough to finally look me in the face. "Like I said, I appreciate what you're saying, but I can see the waters rising, and I really don't see how you're going to get out of this."

Mike turned away and started pulling up some personal pictures that he'd long ago taped to his workstation. He then looked back and gave me a sad smile. "I'm sorry Janet—I do wish you the best, but I have to go."

He wasn't being mean-spirited, just pragmatic, but my own smile quickly disappeared. Mike warily glanced back over at me, and I realized he was probably worried that I might lose it and go off on him. I had been known to slam a few doors from time to time when frustrated, and I certainly knew how to use choice, often heated words in an attempt to motivate anyone who wasn't working as hard or as smart as I thought they could. But I remained calm, and Mike focused once again on his packing effort. As I watched him, I could feel panic rising in my throat. I swallowed hard, hoping to drive down my doubts and bring back the cheerful feeling with which I'd started this conversation.

This was nowhere near the response I expected. Mike had worked for me for a few years, and he was the greatest go-getter of the group, always up for a challenge and always willing to work long hours to win a client or refine a project. He was young and a natural risk-taker. He was a perfect fit for a firm like JANSON, where a creative director can take on more of the role of a partner, and I was sure that he would be there to help me walk through this valley. I expected him to see our current situation as an adventure. We might fall flat on our face, but we also might pull out of this off-kilter position and step up to even greater business and career heights. If Mike wasn't willing to at least try to see where a doubled-down effort might lead, would anybody want to stay?

I soon got my answer. One by one, my employees carefully listened as I told them the situation, and one by one, they wished me luck but told me they had to go.

I watched my employees walk out. I was shocked and disappointed, to be sure, but could I really blame them? It hadn't been that long since I'd been an employee and I understood the tradeoffs that came with that role. Employees performed a clearly defined role in exchange for a paycheck. That contract didn't also require them to take on financial risk.

"Okay, God," I whispered. "I get it. This really isn't going to be easy."

There would be no hiding among the crowd, no one to help shoulder the heavy load. Like someone going through a divorce or through chemotherapy or to prison, I had people around me who cared, who supported me, who wanted to take away the pain and the struggle. But I ultimately would be walking the journey by myself. And that meant I would have to rely completely on Him—and Him alone.

In the moment, I couldn't help but think back to my first salaried job with Orbital Sciences Corporation while I was still a senior in high school.

Ironically, at the time I started, Orbital was a company that, although flush with talent, capital and energy, was facing its own uncertain future.

Of course, I didn't know any of that when I walked in the door that first day. I had no idea who owned it, what they did and what they wanted me to do. Soon, though, Peter, a senior executive, came into the lobby and started providing answers to my unasked questions.

The company, he explained, was in the business of building systems that could take satellites and other payloads into space. It had been started just six years prior by David Thompson, Scott Webster and Bruce Ferguson, who had all met and become friends while getting their MBA degrees at Harvard Business School. Now, they were working on developing a new kind of rocket that could transport small satellites into what was known as low-Earth orbit, or the layer of space located 400 to 1200 miles above the Earth's surface.

At the time, the only organizations that could afford to do this type of work were NASA and their contractors—massive aerospace companies like McDonnell Douglas and Martin Marietta. Building and launching the complex, risky rockets required to boost large-scale satellites into high-Earth orbit required tens of millions of dollars and tens of thousands of man-hours. No one else could play at that level.

Or could they? The folks at tiny, entrepreneurial Orbital were convinced that they could achieve many of the same outcomes with smaller, less expensive launch vehicles. Currently, they were working on a brand-new kind of rocket. Only this one wouldn't take off from a stationary, ground-based launch pad. Instead, it would be attached to the underside of the wing of a large aircraft, flown to an altitude of 40,000 feet (over the ocean) and then dropped. After falling for several seconds, the first-stage rocket would ignite and race off into space, taking its precious payload with it. That was the idea in theory anyway.

Orbital still had to prove it would actually work.

Peter noted that he was working on a major assignment and that he needed someone to take care of all the odds and ends. "You'll be helping me with a bunch of different tasks, like copying, filing, answering my phone, things like that, that I just don't have time for," he stated.

There was no request for a resumé or references. He seemed only to be concerned with making sure that I really wanted the job, not whether I was qualified for it.

He glanced at his watch, clearly eager to get back to work. "Are you ready to start?"

I nodded, trying not to let my excitement bubble over. For $5.50 an hour? Absolutely, I was ready! Peter turned on his heel and led me toward the back offices. As in the lobby, the décor throughout illustrated the company's passion for all things flight. Framed artwork of rockets, lifting towards the heavens, adorned the walls. Lovingly constructed model rockets and model aircraft competed with piles of industry magazines like *Space News*, *Aviation Week* and *Via Satellite* for room on the tops of desks and tables. I couldn't help but be intimidated. My only comparable experience, if you could call it that, was getting hit by a bottle rocket at one of our pool parties.

Peter introduced me to several of my new co-workers, noting that, with my hiring, Orbital's total employee count was now up to 72. It was clear to me that I would also rank as the youngest and, by far, the least educated employee there. Orbital was a hotbed for smart engineers and rocket scientists who hailed from some of the best schools in the country—the Massachusetts Institute of Technology (MIT), CalTech, Virginia Tech—and many of the other employees had advanced, Ivy League degrees in business, marketing and other fields. It was like stumbling into a local Mensa chapter—only the members were considerably cooler. Everyone was so nice, so accepting. They never once made me feel like I didn't belong to the group.

Each day from then on, I waited impatiently for the school day to end so I could race over to Orbital, get to work and do my part to accomplish the mission. I organized. I filed. I typed. I made copies. No task was too mundane or too insignificant for me to give anything less than my absolute best. I loved it!

Peter's project was a temporary one, so as my high school graduation day approached, I assumed that once he was finished, I would be too and then I'd be out of a job. Like most kids, I had been toying with the idea of going away to college, but I'd dragged my feet when it came to getting any applications out. I really had no idea what I wanted to do with my life, and we certainly didn't have the money for me to waste on tuition while I tried to figure it out.

Fortunately, Orbital had other plans. In late May, Bruce Ferguson, one of the three founders who now took care of all the finance and human resource issues, stopped by my work area and offered me a full-time job. He explained that everyone liked my work ethic and my enthusiasm and that I'd be working for Scott Webster, the vice president of marketing, specifically under the supervision of Justin, the marketing manager.

"To be honest, we weren't quite sure what to do with you," Bruce admitted, though he didn't say if that was because of my relative youth or my lack of matriculation plans, or maybe both. "We just know we want you as part of our team."

My response was an unequivocal "Yes!"

Without any planning on my part, I had a career that was taking off. I was still just 17 years old.

Bruce gave me a bona fide title—marketing coordinator—

and, soon, my first supply of business cards. My salary? $13,500 a year. With little financial perspective, I nearly whooped with excitement. This would be a more-than-good-enough living, I thought to myself. I bet I will *never* make more money than this.

My new responsibilities were several steps up from what I had been doing. I would work with Justin and other marketing and PR personnel to develop and distribute various types of promotional and educational materials for the press, potential customers and the general public. That meant helping with everything from putting together press kits to running the logistics and coordination for product rollouts and rocket launches.

It didn't take me long before I too started falling in love with rockets and space.

For the first time, I would be working more closely with some of the top folks at Orbital. This included Dave Thompson, the CEO and clearly the driving force within the company. When it came to technical innovation at Orbital, Dave served as both visionary and detail man, two widely divergent skill sets that would help propel the company forward even in the face of difficult financial pressures, industry skepticism and press attacks.

Like a lot of those from his generation, Dave had witnessed the Space Race and fantasized about one day working for NASA. Unlike most, he achieved his dream job, building advanced rockets at NASA Marshall Space Flight Center. And unlike fewer still, he chose to leave that post not long after he'd started.

It was a risky move, but Dave had begun to believe that the space business shouldn't only be open to the government and its favorite mega-contractors. Like a few other visionaries at that time, he thought that smaller, more nimble and innovative firms could create new commercial applications and cheaper alternatives. Dave enrolled at Harvard Business School to learn the fundamentals and advanced insights needed to start and run a company and soon started hanging with Scott Webster and Bruce Ferguson.

The three friends founded Orbital in April 1982 and started operating it out of what the trio facetiously termed their "world headquarters": a bedroom in the townhouse Dave shared with his wife in southern California.

Their first major project was something called the Transfer Orbit Stage (TOS). Uniquely, it was designed to fit inside the cargo bay of NASA's then relatively new Space Shuttle; once the spacecraft launched and made its way into low-Earth orbit, the TOS, which had its own engines and propellant, would ignite and launch a satellite to its ultimate, higher destination. This project was slated to be the company's bread and butter.

By early 1986, Orbital had moved into high gear managing the construction of the TOS in hopes that it would make its maiden voyage later that year. But then disaster struck. On a frigid January day in Florida, the Space Shuttle Challenger exploded just 73 seconds after liftoff, killing all seven of its crew members. NASA would make radical changes in the wake of the tragedy, not only putting all scheduled Shuttle missions on hold but also ending the use of the Shuttle for any future commercial satellite launches.

For Orbital, it was back to the drawing board. Dave and his team turned their attention to another idea: putting groups of small satellites into low-Earth orbit to enable wireless communications, sensing and navigation. All the company needed was a new type of launch vehicle to actually get them there—and someone to help make it happen.

Fortunately, Dave had a real knack for locating and hiring the right people at the right time. In September of that same year, he brought on a new chief engineer: Antonio Elias, an aeronautical engineer and assistant MIT professor who had worked behind the scenes on the Apollo 16 and Apollo 17 moon landings and had developed an early guidance system for the Space Shuttle.

Antonio immediately began working through the problem of how to ferry and park small satellites in the layer of space just beyond the Earth's atmosphere. He put pencil to paper, doodled a design and ran it back to Orbital. Dave took the torn scratch of legal paper and, as he intently studied the drawing, his eyes began to widen in excitement. Almost immediately, he gave Antonio the green light to move forward. Over the next two years, Orbital poured just about everything it had transforming the sketch drawing into "Pegasus," the winged rocket.

By the summer of 1988, the development of the new launch vehicle was well underway on the west coast, but it was an activity that I was only tangentially aware of. I had just started my full-time job as marketing coordinator, and as I personalized my new work area, I realized that it was time to kick things up a notch.

I was determined to make up for my lack of education and experience through diligence and enthusiasm and by consistently working beyond anyone's expectations of me.

First up: a crash course in aeronautics. Part of my first paycheck went to the purchase of *The Dictionary of Space Technology*. I carried the weighty book with me from work to home and back. I was constantly pulling it out and thumbing through it to find definitions to aeronautic concepts like telemetry, adaptive control systems, geosynchronous orbit and gravitation, along with a deeper understanding of Newton's three laws of motion and why rocket scientists were always referring to them.

Hungry to learn how all of this practically applied to Orbital, I poured over technical papers and trade publications, trying to grasp the inner workings of rocket motors and avionics and how everything worked as one unit. I took copious notes. And I never shied away from asking the smartest people what were probably the dumbest questions they'd ever heard. Amused at but impressed with my earnestness, they would stop what they were doing and try to answer in a way I could understand.

Everything was over my head initially, but I was determined to learn as much as I possibly could, and the leadership at Orbital gave me permission and the freedom to do just that. It was akin to traveling to a foreign land and being totally immersed in the language, culture and customs. Little by little, though, as I read, watched and listened, I began to gain a basic understanding of how all the individual elements worked together to shape the big picture that was Orbital.

Everyone I worked with showed their encouragement and support by trusting me with new challenges and opportunities. My way of thanking them was always to go above and beyond. One day that first summer, Scott Webster, who served as Orbital's head of marketing and business development, came into my office lugging a box of newspaper and magazine clippings. Together, these contained every mention of an Orbital activity and every quote provided by an Orbital executive over the prior three years.

"Organize these for me, please," he directed. He gave me no other instructions, and Justin, a nervous sort who was focused on his own projects and deadlines, waved me off and told me to take care of it however I saw fit.

I wrestled the box onto the top of my desk, and one by one laid each article out around me before moving to the floor to give myself more room.

As I browsed the various headlines, I decided to get creative. The three founders had a healthy parent-like pride in their company and its accomplishments, so I was determined to make a guide that would allow them to easily reference all the various media coverage. I made copies and organized every clip by publication and date, placed them into plastic sleeves and then into three-ring binders. On opening the book, the men could look through a table of contents, as well an appendix that featured each article by category, title, date, publication and journalist. I worked well into the night to get it all just right.

The next morning, I walked into Scott Webster's office and handed him three books, one each for 1985, 1986 and 1987. "Sir, here are your notebooks."

"What's this?" he asked, genuinely perplexed.

"Those are all your news clippings. I organized them," I explained. "I made one each for Dave and Bruce as well. Now you can all just look through and see yourself in the news whenever you want."

He glanced at the title on the cover of the top book, opened it and began flipping through the pages. Halfway through, a big grin took over his face. "Janet, we weren't expecting this," he said. "This is fantastic!"

His approving words washed over me, and I couldn't wait for my next project. Whatever anyone asked me to do I jumped on, pouring myself into the work. I was in the trenches doing mostly grunt work, but it gave me a bottoms-up appreciation for every obscure but still important detail that went into fundamentally strong marketing and product development initiatives.

I turned 18 late that summer, and I was slowly finding my place in the real world. Orbital was the perfect place for a hard-working, ambitious kid like myself. It was so exciting, this field I'd stumbled into, where I was surrounded by people who valued me, the same people who I respected and admired and who were willing to give me chance after chance to prove myself and succeed.

Like many older teens finding their own way, though, I found myself slowly drifting away from my core values. Oh, I still went to church. I prayed every once in a while, typically when I needed something. But I had morphed largely into a check-the-box Christian, holding God at arm's length. I wanted Him close enough just in case I needed Him, but mostly I was off doing my own thing. And my own thing at that point was Orbital.

As 1989 dawned, the marketing workload at Orbital began to increase exponentially. Pegasus was scheduled to launch in August, and my boss wanted to start building a sense of anticipation within the press and among potential investors.

An undercurrent of excitement pervaded the atmosphere, and we all worked hard refining our invitation list and guest operations, working the phones to confirm attendance and developing press and technical packets.

One day in June, Justin told me to go home early and pack my bags. We were heading to California and the NASA Dryden Flight Research Center,[2] where Orbital had built a hangar and was assembling and testing Pegasus. The marketing team's task

2 On March 1, 2014, NASA renamed its Dryden Flight Research Center the Armstrong Flight Research Center in honor of Neil Armstrong, a test pilot, Apollo 11 astronaut and the first man to walk on the moon.

was to pull together the unveiling of a "mock" Pegasus for the press and various dignitaries.

My first thought? I get to see the Pacific Ocean! We were on a tight schedule and Justin, whose anxiety had now reached off-the-chart levels, wasn't too keen on getting off track. Still, he acquiesced after I harassed him nearly the entire flight, promising to make a quick detour on the way to our destination.

After landing at the Los Angeles airport, he steered our rental car off of the main thoroughfare and past what felt like a hundred stoplights before pulling up alongside a public beach.

"Okay," Justin said, shoving the gear shaft into park, "you've got 10 minutes. Enjoy."

I jumped out and felt a rush of pure bliss as I gazed out over the swelling expanse of water. In the distance, I could see surfers bobbing up and down on their boards, even as a lone seagull invaded my view, diving headfirst toward a towering wave before pulling up short and flying out. I knelt to run my fingers through the sandy beach and took in another drawn-out look at the ocean beyond. Too soon, though, I heard a car horn blow impatiently.

Though an open window, Justin hollered, "Time to go!"

I gulped two deep breaths of salty air and hopped back into the car.

"Thanks," I said, meaning it.

Justin nodded, a brief smile crossing his face as he put the car back into drive. He zipped back through the crowded streets of Los Angeles and soon picked up the 405, speeding east towards the hot, dusty Mojave Desert and the Dryden Flight Research Center and easily making up the time I'd pilfered from our schedule.

The unveiling ceremony of Pegasus went even better than we all hoped. Everyone marveled at the replica of the new launch vehicle and its sleek, white, compound carbon exterior. It looked like nothing anyone in the rocket business had ever seen. From a distance and especially in the air, it resembled a flying salmon, with three fins on its tail and a single, large, triangular wing located on the top and positioned approximately three-quarters of the way down its 49-foot-long fuselage. The unconventional design gave the vehicle the lift it would need to power up when ignited in mid-air and the stability to fly perfectly straight even as G-forces squeezed in from all sides. I stood on the periphery of the crowd, handing out technical packets filled with Pegasus's unique specifications.

Around me, I could hear murmurs of genuine excitement. People recognized that they were looking at an innovation that could change the trajectory of commercial space ventures. If it worked, Pegasus would be the first new launch vehicle developed in the U.S. in nearly two decades.

Back at Orbital, the ride was about to get bumpy. The original August launch date was pushed back another seven months, and then it was pushed back another month. Despite the delays, everyone worked hard to stay focused on the mission. It was amazing to witness, this cadre of very smart, very passionate people all coming together to achieve the mission, one single-minded purpose that was greater than any one person. Pegasus was everyone's project, whether someone was building it, promoting it and keeping track of the expenses.

The offices seemed to hum and crackle with excitement, and everyone worked to keep their anticipation under control even as we all began to count down the months, the weeks and then the days to launch.

In late March 1990, the PR and marketing teams, myself

included, headed back to California to coordinate with NASA on how best to film the launch and handle publicity. Soon after that, many of the company's other employees followed. For those lucky enough to be there, it was a chance to reunite with the Pegasus team members who had spent months living in almost complete isolation in the California desert as they built and perfected their "baby."

The day finally came in early April for Pegasus to show the world what it could do. That morning, the sun rose so brightly that the glare made it almost impossible to make out the spiky Joshua Trees dotting the desert landscape. We were "Go for Launch!"

The crew climbed into the massive B-52 carrying Pegasus. Behind it was a NASA chase plane, which would film the launch and relay back a live feed. As the B-52 took off from the runway and began its long ascent to a position 43,000 feet above the Pacific Ocean just southwest of Monterey, we all made our way to the established viewing area. Orbital and NASA employees, along with industry contractors, elected officials and the press, milled about in nervous anticipation.

Finally, the two planes completed their climb to the stratosphere and moved into position. Standing off to the side of the viewing room, I thought I would drop before Pegasus did. I gripped a colleague's arm to steady myself and then held my breath as the launch vehicle plunged off the wing of the B-52, falling silently towards the ocean below. Several members of the design group stood straight up as Pegasus momentarily disappeared from the screen. The camera switched to a different angle, bringing Pegasus clearly into view. The rocket was still holding its horizontal position and plummeting. Everyone began silently counting down the seconds.

5...4...3...2...1....Right on time, the boosters ignited and Pegasus leapt forward, its tail fins sinking down as its nose rose, bucking, thrusting and zooming its way skyward. The rocket rapidly accelerated to 5,800 miles per hour. The entire crowd suddenly erupted, clapping, cheering and rooting Pegasus on. I knew at that moment that I was seeing history in the making. Soon, Pegasus's second-stage boosters lit, propelling the vehicle to speeds of more than 17,000 miles per hour. She rapidly disappeared from our screens, punching through the ozone and continuing on to the thermosphere to deliver her dual multi-million-dollar payload: a military communications satellite and a NASA scientific satellite.

Nine minutes after launch, a voice came through the loud-speaker, announcing: "Pegasus is in orbit."

The celebration hit a new decibel level as if we'd just won the Super Bowl at the last second. Dave's vision had come to fruition. His belief had been redeemed. He had insisted that America could get to space faster and cheaper and he'd just written the "how to" on a new way to make it happen. Pegasus was the first launch vehicle successfully developed in 20 years, and it would dramatically change the space business.

"We said we would do it and we did it," Dave told the large gaggle of reporters bustling around him in the NASA pressroom. "Today's launch will make it more likely that customers with defense, scientific and commercial purposes will come forward."

Over to the side, I tried to process it all. I was 19 years old and had been a witness to aeronautical history, even playing my own small part. It wasn't on the order of a moon landing, but it would be a pivotal moment in the chronicles of commercial space, opening the door to an increasingly connected, data-driven and mobile society. A year later, the Pegasus team would travel to the White House, where President George H.W. Bush awarded them the National Medal of Technology.

Everything changed after that. The pace got even quicker. Orbital's leadership decided to go public with a multi-million dollar stock offering. And I got a new boss: Leslie, the vice president and general counsel who already oversaw the legal department. She would take over both the marketing and public relations departments.

With a wardrobe that included St. John business suits and perfectly coiffed hair, Leslie was impressive and brilliant, a strong strategic thinker and a whiz with mergers and acquisitions. But she was also one "tough cat" who refused to tolerate much nonsense from anyone. She "owned" her role as head of our department and she also "owned" her seat in the boardroom.

I worried whether I would be up to her standards—and, in clipped tones, she let me know soon enough that I wasn't. "You can do better, Janet," she would admonish me.

Fortunately, I wasn't alone in dealing with these stringent expectations. My best friend, Laura, who was the manager of PR, also worked for Leslie, and we settled into a new routine of publicizing Pegasus and Orbital's growing business. It was a huge task.

As marketing coordinator, I helped support all the publicity around launch events. This included making sure we had all the promotional items ordered, like Pegasus mugs, Pegasus hats, and Pegasus launch patches; pulling together invitation lists for dignitaries and other launch guests; and getting an official photographer and videographer on scene to capture Pegasus on the tarmac and in flight.

As I spent more time with Leslie, I started to see that beneath the tough exterior was a caring person. Over time, she became a mentor, and like many others at Orbital, she would play an important part in molding me into a young business professional. I never lost sight of the fact that I was blessed to be surrounded by very smart, hardworking men and women who were willing to teach me, give me increasingly important responsibilities and opportunities and shape my trajectory so that it was always pointed up.

And I made the most of it. Though I liked to joke and have fun with friends and colleagues, I never went through a big partying phase in my early adulthood. Instead, I remained laser-focused on learning as much as could and taking on every project my boss and others were willing to give me. And much of that was because at Orbital, I didn't feel average. The people inspired me and the work challenged me, bringing out skills and capabilities that I didn't realize I had, and through it all I began to get an inkling of the deep complexities—the right personnel, the in-depth knowledge, the perfect timing—required to actually achieve success in this industry. Each launch, each project, was a scientific wonder, and I felt privileged to be a part of the Orbital mission. I played only a small role, but it was a role that I was determined to play to the absolute best of my ability.

By that summer, Leslie began encouraging me to pursue a college degree. Once she realized that I was willing, she discussed it with Dave. They agreed that Orbital would pick up the tab for all of my tuition, books and fees—so long as I maintained a 3.5 grade point average, kept up my current workload and committed to remaining at Orbital for three years after graduation.

In the fall of 1990, I enrolled at Strayer College with plans to major in business and minor in marketing. Uniquely, the school offered nighttime classes and support for working students. The academics and the many classroom discussions helped expand my understanding of business and marketing fundamentals and sharpened the critical skills that I would need in my career at Orbital and eventually in my business. Truly, though, it was my time on the front lines at Orbital that gave me my real education.

My already busy schedule became grueling. In the early 1990s, Orbital grew from less than one hundred employees to several thousand. The rocket launch schedule was packed, and not just for Pegasus. In 1993, Orbital's TOS vehicle finally went to space aboard the Space Shuttle Discovery, and the company soon began developing new rockets and satellite systems and acquiring other companies.

I became a frequent traveler, not only for Pegasus launch events but also domestic and international aerospace trade shows. I got to go to New York, Cape Canaveral, Spain, Dubai and the Netherlands. I executed Orbital's event management and communications activities at Kennedy Space Center for the launch of the Mars Observer, which was designed to study and take high-resolution photographs of the Martian surface but required a TOS ride to propel it into high enough orbit to start the voyage towards the Red Planet. I rubbed elbows with high-level officials from NASA and foreign space agencies. I had an on-the-ground view of the Space Shuttle lifting off, along with other famous rocket systems like the Atlas, Delta and Titan.

Not wanting to waste any part of the opportunity, I continued to try to learn more, not just about Orbital's business but also the burgeoning global space market, including commercial space and military space. I asked a ton of questions and signed up to sit in on as many presentations as I could, even if they were well above my pay grade. At a conference in the

Netherlands, for example, I attended an educational session about the potential for satellites equipped with remote sensing capabilities. This technology, I learned, could measure ocean temperatures, radiance (or ocean light) or even algal blooms to better forecast weather and determine fish concentrations—data that had huge implications for a number of industries, including commercial fishing.

It was a mind-boggling experience for anyone, much less someone just entering their 20s, and the pressure was on to maintain the highest possible standards, both at work and at school.

My mother would always support me where she could, cooking me hot meals when I made it home early enough in the evening and running errands for me when time was especially tight. My instructors were extraordinarily gracious in their will-ingness to accommodate my unique needs. When I traveled, I would call my professor upon my arrival, and he or she would fax me the quiz or test, no matter how late it was in their time zone. I would sit down, fill out the answers, fax it back and, without missing a beat, return to my Orbital work.

In late spring of 1995, I finally received my bachelor's de-gree, and Mom threw me a graduation party. Many of my colleagues from Orbital attended, including Dave and his wife. I was truly touched. Dave was now the CEO of one of the most dynamic, successful companies in the aerospace industry and routinely worked and socialized with famous, influential people in Washington, and yet he made it a point to attend my graduation party.

He also came with a gift: a promotion. I was now manager of corporate communications at Orbital, continuing my upward climb in an industry that seven years ago I knew absolutely nothing about and never would have chosen for myself.

How had I gotten here? For the first time in a long while, I thought about God's providence. If my mother had not insisted that I stay at my school, if she had left it up to me, I never would have been in the school office when Orbital called and I would have missed a blessing that God had waiting for me. I had been in the right place at the right time. It was not my doing or my timing, but God's doing and God's timing. Once again, He had taken the bad circumstances of my life and brought an abundance of good out of them. The question remained: Was I going to use this gift for my own purposes or for His?

At that point, I couldn't even begin to say. Orbital was like the first-stage rocket that had launched me on my way, only I still didn't know exactly where I was heading. That would soon change.

FOUR

BAD FAITH, GOOD FAITH

Trust in the Lord with all your heart, and lean not on your own understanding; in all your ways acknowledge Him, and He shall direct your paths. Proverbs 3:5-6

The evening after my employees left, I found myself sitting on a plane bound for Florida and a major industry trade show. As the plane lifted from the runway, I looked out to see dark skies cloaking Washington, D.C., and its sprawling suburbs as wind and rain pelted the window. I gripped the armrest to calm my nerves as the aircraft bounced every which way in its singled-minded struggle to rise above the weather. At the moment, I couldn't help equating the harsh turbulence as an apt metaphor for the current state of my own life and career.

The day had once again started with me furiously tapping my pencil on my desk as I grappled with how best to move forward. In particular, I couldn't decide whether or not I should even consider taking this trip.

The timing could not have been worse. The pieces that I needed to start picking up were more than overwhelming at this point. There were ongoing client projects that I needed to sort out and reassign to freelance writers and designers even as deadlines loomed and unpaid bills continued to pile up.

Attending the trade show wasn't a paying gig; there would be no invoice of carefully listed tasks and hours to remit. The value was less tangible and more long-term: a chance to meet face to face with my clients, network with key industry players and educate myself about market breakthroughs and opportunities within the industry. The trip might indirectly affect the bottom line at some unknown point in the future—and then again it might not. On the other hand, everything was already paid for, the plane and conference tickets non-refundable. In normal times, I would have been eager to go. But now? It seemed like an indulgence.

I stopped tapping long enough to bow my head and say a short prayer for guidance. *What should I do, Lord? Go or stay?* When I opened my eyes, the answer came to me quickly. I'd already decided to carry on with my business, no matter what. In healthier times, I'd go to the trade show, no questions asked. It was part and parcel of doing business in this industry. If I truly believed that God wanted JANSON to survive, I needed to show my faith by my actions, not just my words.

Quickly gathering my tickets and some client files, I left my mother in charge to man the phones and drove home to pack, throwing a few business suits and some comfortable shoes into my garment bag before heading for the airport. I knew it would be difficult to set aside my worries, but I dug down deep, and the next morning, as I walked into the conference center, I thought I was doing a pretty good job of acting upbeat and positive.

A mix of government and private sector attendees milled about the many booths displaying the latest technologies and products while waiting for the time when the keynote speakers and others would take to the stage inside of a nearby auditorium. Coffee in hand, I slipped into the crowd and began wandering through the exhibit area, on the lookout for the faces of my clients.

It didn't take me long. One of the first clients I ran into was Bea, president of a major government contractor. For most of her life she'd been a stay-at-home mom who enjoyed sewing cheerleader uniforms and patching Girl Scout tents, but at 43 years old, she got the entrepreneurial bug. BMI was now a flourishing business that manufactured portable shelters for the Department of Defense.

Bea lit up when she saw me. "Janet!" she said warmly. "I was hoping you'd make it."

JANSON provided a small amount of marketing work for her company from time to time, but early on I'd asked Bea to serve as one of JANSON's business advisers. One reason was that she was one of only a few women executives working in the industry and I needed the input of someone like that. Another reason was that she had some serious drive.

Bea showed me one of her latest military shelters on display within her booth. The tent was outfitted with built-in electrical wires and made out of a unique material that made it literally invisible to the enemy at night. Then we talked some about how the U.S. military action in Afghanistan and the post-9/11 environment were affecting demand for her products.

Inevitably, though, she asked how I was doing. She knew things were not good, as she was one of the few people I'd phoned to confide the potential devastation JANSON was facing. She'd been encouraging on the phone, but now she placed her hand on my arm and smiled at me as if to will away the negative thoughts that had probably started clouding my face.

"Janet," she said kindly, "there are always going to be ups and down in your business. Don't let anyone tell you that you can't handle it. Just stay focused on the business."

I thanked her. I know she meant well and it was sound advice, but I just couldn't take it in. Physically, I was here in Florida working my business, but I really wasn't, at least not in any way that counted. Even as she continued to try to encourage me, my mind just kept going over and over what I'd done, what I hadn't done, what I should have done. I was fixated on my failures, not my future. It reminded me of how people try so hard to boost you up after a breakup: "There are plenty of fish in the sea," they say, or "You're such a lovable person; of course, you'll meet someone else"—when all you can think is, *I just want things to go back to the way they were.*

The fact was, I was in shock and denial. I was still grieving the loss of any sense of normalcy I once had—even if my business and finances had been a mess. I wanted to focus on the future, but I really couldn't envision a future at this point, couldn't imagine what it would take to turn it all around. It was easier to keep looking back and fixate on my inadequacies and what I had lost.

I shook my shoulders, as if to throw off the heavy thoughts. The least I could do is go through the motions, so I forced myself to meet with clients. I inspected their latest products and got up to speed on their latest concerns. I sat in on educational sessions. And I spent time talking to and getting to know new people in the industry. By the end of the day, I had almost convinced myself that this was going to be a truly positive experience.

Until the next morning. As I headed onto the show floor for the second day of networking, I rounded a corner and then stopped suddenly, not completely sure I was seeing right. There they were: several of my former employees, including Mike!

They all stood next to each other in deep conversation with a representative of a prospective client. *What the heck are they doing?* I thought, taking in two deep breaths to try to slow the rush of adrenaline shooting towards my feet. Shopping their resumés? Hardly.

As I took a step closer and ducked behind a pole, I could hear them making a business pitch. The narrative sounded awfully familiar. It soon became obvious that they had, in a matter of fewer than three days, somehow launched their own marketing firm—only the services were identical to JANSON's and, except for a word here and there, so too was their elevator pitch. In hindsight, I now realized that Mike had been too calm, too rehearsed when I had spoken to him a few days earlier. He and the others had all made the potentially life-changing decision to walk out on their jobs and responsibility with too much haste, too little distress. It didn't matter that I had argued the merits of fighting for the company. Their perception was that neither JANSON nor I would survive this, and so they were getting positioned to catch the fleeing clients that would be ripe for the taking.

I sucked in a quick, loud breath and leaned forward as if the recognition of betrayal had been a physical stab to the heart. *Oh God, help me hold it together,* I pleaded.

I looked up and saw that Mike and his conspirators were on the move, making their way down the row of booths toward the auditorium. I picked up my things and rounded back, speed-walking the next aisle over. I waited at the end of their row and when I saw them coming, casually stepped forward, blocking their path. They halted in mid-step and stared. Mike opened his mouth as if to say something but then suddenly closed it and looked down at his feet. It must have never occurred to any of them that I would actually make the trip. He looked up and then directly at me with a pinched look of arrogance and defiance mixed with shame.

"Un-be-lievable," I spat. "Simply unbelievable."

It hurt to think that anyone, much less the people I had brought into my world, the ones I saw as my battle buddies, would actually be rooting for me to fail. Didn't they understand how much I'd put into starting my own company? Didn't they realize the risks I'd been willing to take? I had spent years thinking and praying about it, doing my homework, talking to industry colleagues and planning before I actually made the move to start JANSON—but I had been above-board and transparent with my employer. I had done everything in good faith, not bad.

The journey from initial idea to company kickoff had started years before while I was still working at Orbital Sciences Corporation. By then, I'd received my marketing degree from Strayer College and become the manager of corporate communications. The workload within the marketing department was especially intense because Orbital was in the midst of a major growth spurt.

Dave Thompson, the co-founder and CEO, wasn't content with just developing a revolutionary launch vehicle like Pegasus. He wanted his company to keep reaching higher. In the early 1990s, he tasked his team of engineers with developing a ground-based rocket that could put even larger payloads into low-Earth orbit. With the market for wireless communications exploding, Dave and the leadership team also expanded the company's ability to manufacture small satellites by acquiring a competitor, Fairchild Space and Defense Corporation. This purchase not only enabled Orbital to finally start catching up with all the satellite orders that were pouring in, but it doubled the company's employee rolls.

As time went by, there were even more acquisitions in the works as Dave pressed forward with his vision to provide complex constellations of low-Earth satellites that could enable cutting-edge capabilities like satellite-to-ground tracking services, weather forecasting and a variety of defense and intelligence applications.

All of these moves served to keep me and my marketing and public relations colleagues hopping. We were constantly working to revise Orbital's marketing materials and events to make sure that we were always communicating the absolute latest and greatest on Orbital's advancements. I was still responsible for coordinating logistics and marketing support for launch events, but my new job also required me to take a much deeper role in creating the annual report and marketing materials for the new divisions of the company. For these tasks, I started working closely with Jeff Lawson, a tall, clean-cut, easygoing sort who was an incredibly talented graphics designer.

Orbital wasn't just growing, it was growing up. It was now a well-known, highly respected industry leader listed on the NASDAQ stock exchange with multiple divisions and multiple locations. Company executives determined that it was time for Orbital to elevate its brand image by launching a nationwide advertising campaign. To do so, though, we needed to look beyond the marketing department and hire a full-service advertising agency.

The budget? $500,000.

To us, that seemed like a pretty nice chunk of change, and we were sure the various advertising agencies would be jostling to win Orbital's business. We wanted to give everyone a fair shot, but we also wanted to do our due diligence and make sure that whichever agency we contracted with had the creative chops and the internal culture to effectively show and tell the Orbital story through design, photography and narrative.

Through our research, we narrowed the list down to six agencies and then reached out and asked each to submit a creative and financial proposal. I was especially eager to see the different creative concepts the agencies came up with, but then a strange thing happened. One by one, instead of proposals, Orbital got short, pithy letters...rejection letters! That was a new one, to be sure. The potential payees were turning down the payer. In the end, all but one of the firms voluntarily took themselves out of the running; actually, they never even entered the starting gate.

Each communiqué was a variation on the same theme: not enough money. Those that rejected us had a bottom-line benchmark: They wouldn't open their door to an account worth less than $1 million. Orbital was not only not in the ballpark, they were down the street, stuck in the parking lot.

So, by default, Orbital got itself an advertising agency. The only firm that sent us a proposal and was willing to take us on was smaller than the others. But they had been in business for decades and they turned out to be wonderful people. We all loved their creativity and we loved working with them. Still, unlike the larger agencies on our list, they didn't have much experience in the aerospace market and they struggled to fully understand what we did and the nuances of our market. They didn't speak our language or really get what Orbital was all about, so how could they possibly tell a compelling story about us?

For the first time, I realized how much of the "narrative" I had absorbed and internalized over the years. It had been the result of years of reading, of listening to and talking with engineers, executives, customers and advertising trade representatives, of getting an on-the-ground view of the challenges that customers faced, of seeing the products and services in action. Little by little, I had begun (somewhat unknowingly) to weave all this knowledge into a tapestry of details and color that could inform an impactful message and communications strategy.

I had fallen in love with Orbital's story, and at that moment I realized, if you don't know or believe in the story, then you can't bring out its value. And that is exactly what we needed the industry to realize in this advertising campaign: Orbital's value.

What I had learned at Orbital couldn't be picked up by reading a brochure or a few press articles. The ad agency was working the best way they knew how, but it wasn't enough. And so the Orbital marketing team spent hours filling in knowledge gaps and putting the final touches on a campaign that would meet Dave's expectations.

At some point, this whole exercise began to reveal something greater to me. Could there be a market for a niche communications firm that specialized in the aerospace market? Perhaps so. Obviously, the larger agencies were happy to take care of the well-established, Tier 1 firms with plenty of connections and plenty of money. But what about the smaller, up-and-coming firms? By this time, there were hundreds of these Tier 2 and Tier 3 businesses coming into the industry and they too would also struggle to find a marketing firm that understood their market well enough to define their differentiator, to effectively tell their story.

The experience we'd just gone through had been frustrating, but maybe this was the silver lining. I knew the aerospace market: the players, the lexicon, the unique marketing dynamics, the trends and the other market intricacies that were constantly changing.

I could provide real value to a smaller aerospace company that needed to differentiate itself, to brand itself, to tell its story, to relay its value. And I would be more than happy to do it for $500,000, or even $100,000 or $50,000.

The thought nagged at me constantly, whether I was sitting at home, doing research or traveling to another launch event. I was just 27 years old, but I knew deep down that this was an idea that had legs. I started praying about it and talking to my close industry colleagues.

As my career with Orbital continued to soar, my personal and spiritual lives began also slowly to fall into place. I had bought a townhouse and was living on my own. I had plenty of good friends. And although everything seemed to be going my way naturally, I now recognized that I did need God to play an active role in my life.

While at Orbital, life revolved around striving and succeeding and keeping up with what were increasingly showy appearances. I got caught up in it at times. I loved the work, but sometimes I also came home feeling empty and wanting more depth, more meaning in my life.

I began to seek God out and not in a shallow or cursory way, not just to "look" like a good Christian. Church once again became an important aspect of my life, but church wasn't the end goal, it was just an avenue. What I really was focused on was having a "personal" relationship with Jesus and growing in that relationship. I wanted to grow in my understanding of Him.

The change in heart led to a change in activities. Jumping

at the chance to practice my public speaking skills, I had volunteered to narrate the annual Christmas drama. And one of the pastors had recently asked me to start teaching a Sunday School class for working women.

Through it all, I couldn't help but notice that I was maturing, both as a person and as a Christian. I was no longer just a Baptist by virtue of birth. I found myself increasingly willing to at least consult God before making any major decisions in my life. Soon enough, I started consulting him on the minor items too.

I began to pray for guidance on whether, how and when to start my own business. The answers didn't come immediately, and there were days when I thought I was a bit crazy even to consider leaving my full-time job. Orbital had been a Godsend in so many ways: a starting point that had taken me up the corporate ladder at a young age, a major ingredient in my still-fragile identity.

At the same time, I faced a dilemma: Unless I went back to school to get an MBA, I felt that my progression at Orbital was essentially in a holding pattern. And even if I did make that big investment of time and money, was I made for this mission?

Life had been great at Orbital. The work was incredible, I'd been on some amazing business trips and I had wonderful friends and colleagues that I got to work with. Being a part of that team had been, pardon the pun, "a blast." We worked exceptionally hard and spent a lot of hours on the mission, but we were also determined to make it as fun as possible. And we did!

But Orbital was a different company now, still innovative, still cutting-edge, but more corporate, more bureaucratic and not quite as vibrant. It had gone through the same natural evolution that would have occurred in any company that had skyrocketed from fewer than 100 employees to somewhere around 5,000. It wasn't better or worse, just different, and I needed to find the answer to this question: Was this really where I was supposed to be?

When my mother got wind of my thinking, she couldn't believe it. "That company has been so good to you, Jan. Why in the world would you want to jeopardize that?" she asked.

She had come up in an age when you went to work for a company and, unless you were laid off or retired, you stayed. She wondered how I could possibly be willing to risk all the security that came with a full-time job, in particular, the very generous opportunities that Orbital had given me.

"You had really better think this through, Jan," she admonished, hoping to scare some sense into me. "Your future is set. Don't go and blow it."

When my entrepreneurial ponderings continued beyond her comfort zone, she moved to an even more direct approach. "Seriously, Jan, if I were you, I would *not* leave that company."

All of her arguments were fair, her concerns reasonable, and I took them under advisement, but the thought just wouldn't go away. It was so persistent. It often woke me in the middle of the night, and as I began to have serious conversations with others in the industry, my confidence started to take hold. And the more I prayed, the more I began to feel a sense of peace that this path was the one I was supposed to take, that this was what God wanted me to do.

I was eager to exercise the risk and I was eager to let my entrepreneurial spirit fly free. It was not that I thought I could make the best lemonade in the business—I had no intention of trying to compete with the biggest agencies for the biggest companies. What I knew I could make and sell was some very good lemonade to a very specific market—the Tier 2 and Tier 3 aerospace companies.

I also realized that I couldn't go it alone. About a year into this period, I called Jeff to my office. I could take care of the marketing, the sales, the client interface and the project management, but I needed somebody to provide the creative side of the business. Jeff, to my mind, was the perfect choice. He was so talented and knowledgeable, and we already had a strong working relationship established.

It didn't take long before Jeff ambled into my fifth-floor office. "Hey, what's going on?" he asked. I'm sure he was expecting me to detail a new assignment or ask his advice about something that was already in the works.

"Sit down," I said, gesturing for him to take a seat in front of my desk. "I've got this idea, and I want to see what you think about it."

I told him that I wanted to start a small marketing communications company that would focus on the smaller and unique needs of aerospace companies. His eyes widened, and his forehead crinkled, but he didn't say anything. I couldn't tell if he was intrigued or shocked, so I kept going. I explained how the experience with the advertising project had revealed a potentially gaping hole in the market and I detailed my plan for creating a niche company that could fill that gap. Then I told him that I wanted him to be part of it.

His eyes got even bigger. "We work really well together already," I said quickly. "You're so good with the creative stuff. I'm good with the marketing and customer management side. I think we could make it and maybe make it big."

I tried to read his thoughts, but he didn't make me work too hard at it. "Let's do it," he said suddenly. "I love it!"

"Really?" I said. "Oh, wow! Fantastic! Well, let's both start thinking about a name for the company."

On Monday morning, Jeff beat me to it. Smiling broadly, he walked into my office and laid out some materials on my desk.

"What's this?" I asked.

He had a name, JANSON, he announced proudly: "JAN" for Janet and "SON" for Lawson. And he had created a logo.

We were ready for business, but there still was one small obstacle. We had no clients, no path forward. It would have been insane to quit our jobs cold turkey, so we agreed that we would take baby steps. We would start out part-time, see how it all went and, if and when sales started coming in, Jeff would resign. Then, if revenues continued to grow, I would follow.

I needed to talk to my boss and ask for some flexibility in my job. I wanted to do everything in good faith, so I was upfront about my business idea. "If I keep up with all my projects and responsibilities, could I work four long days a week instead of five?" I asked. Surprisingly, she wasn't against the idea. Maybe she saw me like the orphaned child raised in a convent who needed to venture outside the walls and see what she might be missing out on before making the full commitment to a nun's life.

"Yes," she said. "But you do realize that this is just some phase you're going through."

She said it as a fact, not a question. But she gave me what I had asked for, and it was incredibly generous. In fact, I didn't realize it fully at the time, but what a blessing that I could be so upfront with my employer. How many employees could walk into their boss's office, announce their plan to eventually start their own company and actually keep their jobs? Not that many, I'm sure.

As such, there was no need to counter her point. Maybe we would fail, but I had to try at least. It was an attitude that I'd picked up from working at Orbital. *Think big, dream big*.

So Jeff and I spent all of our off-hours, including evenings and weekends, working on JANSON. We shopped for the computers, printers, desks, phones and office supplies we would need, setting up workable offices in our respective homes and identifying clients we could go after. In short order, we'd run up $6,000 on the corporate credit card we'd secured. *Yikes!* I remember thinking. *Will we ever be able to pay this thing off?*

In short order, our efforts started to reap a small harvest of business, although it was just basic marketing work for medical offices and small local companies: logos, brochures, websites. It wasn't on target with our mission, but it gave us a portfolio of work to show off and references to cite. Before long, we started to make inroads within the aerospace industry, and soon after that, we were designing full branding packages for small, local players. All of it helped cover the cost of our equipment and operating costs, and eventually, we had enough income for Jeff to resign and start working for JANSON full-time. We were, however, not even close to bringing in enough for me to make the break for independence.

I made it a point to work my network even harder. Since I had established good friendships with the advertising reps within the aerospace and defense trade media, I stayed in tight communications with them and asked for referrals. One of those friends lived in San Francisco and sold ads for several leading industry publications. One day she called and gave me an unbelievable tip. One of the largest aerospace companies in the industry was looking for a new marketing firm.

I reached out to Renee, the company's marketing manager, and she agreed to give me a meeting. Because I was still working four days a week at Orbital, I had to make the trip on a Friday, catching the 6 a.m. flight to San Francisco. I changed into my business wardrobe in the ladies' bathroom at the airport, grabbed a car and headed to their headquarters in the heart of California's Silicon Valley. There, in a large, airy conference room, I met Renee and the company's vice president of marketing.

As I began my presentation, I was both nervous and confident. I played up my market knowledge and how it would benefit them. I showed a variety of examples of our creative work. They asked a lot of questions and I had no problem providing the answers.

When I was finished, they thanked me and told me they'd be back in touch the following week. Trying not to draw any conclusions about which direction they might be leaning, I drove back to the airport and then took the red-eye flight home.

On Monday, I tapped my pencil restlessly, willing the phone to ring even though I knew it could be days, if not weeks, before I heard anything. Fortunately, they didn't make me wait long. At noon, which was 9 a.m. California time, Renee called. It was official: The company wanted JANSON to be their marketing agency.

I let out a big whoop and called to tell Jeff.

The account, which came with a lofty annual advertising budget and would bring in additional revenue for our creative work, was a breakthrough. It would provide us with what is known in the industry as a "house account," the strong foundation of ongoing work and cash flow that we needed to fully launch. It would also require so much of my attention that I had no choice but to leave my full-time job.

I was poised but a little emotional when I walked in to give my resignation. Orbital had given me my start, the "boot camp" training I needed to grow and thrive in this industry, and I would walk away with great memories and the highest level of respect for everyone involved. The company's willingness to give this type of opportunity to an unproven kid like myself had changed everything for me on so many levels. And Dave had been my entrepreneurial role model, never showing fear, always pushing the envelope, open declaring his vision and then going out and getting it done. I was so grateful, and I could feel myself tearing up when he graciously wished me well. "You always have a place here, Janet," Dave told me as I left his office.

I had learned so much at Orbital, but it was time to learn more and moving forward was necessary.

Surprisingly, my mother had also come around to the rightness of my decision. When I went to her home later that evening to let her know that I had submitted my resignation to Orbital, she shocked me with her response. "Well, Jan, I really didn't want you to do this, but I know you've prayed about it and I believe that you will do well."

That meant everything to me. As usual, she would end up being JANSON's biggest cheerleader—in good times and bad.

So, as I walked away from the trade show that day, I resolved to fight for my company. JANSON wasn't a concept birthed overnight. It came about after a lot of thought, prayer, discussion, collaboration and hard work. But now the time had come for me to exercise a role in which I had not yet been battled tested: managing through adversity. And that required me to step out in faith and accept that my once smooth path was now laden with a lot of potholes, bumps and bends. When you're in the valley, you have to start moving, and the sooner the better; in my case, though, any effort to rescue my company's success was going to happen at a crawl-walk pace, not a run. But it is often on this uncertain, uncomfortable path where we learn some of life's greatest lessons.

I thought of Habakkuk 3:19, which says, "He will make our feet like deer feet and set us on the high hill."

To get to the top of the hill, though, I still had to make my way up the valley and start climbing the steep slope on the far end.

I sat down, mindlessly took another sip of my now lukewarm coffee and watched as business dealings on the show floor continued on as usual.

It was time for me to quit staring backward and make a path forward. I just needed to doggedly start putting one foot in front of the other.

— FIVE —

STARTING OVER, "AGAIN"

*...Forgetting those things which are behind and reaching forward
to those things which are ahead.* Philippians 3:13

One of the first rules of crisis management is to take control
of the story. I knew I needed to get out in front of this
situation and fast. Without hearing from me, clients would have
no choice but to believe that JANSON was in real trouble and
possibly start looking for a new marketing company.

After taking a few deep gulps of air, I called a freelance writer
who regularly worked for JANSON. Though she wasn't on staff,
she was dependable, a calming presence in the midst of any
form of chaos. I could always count on her to provide unique
insights on how to craft a message for the target audience, using
all the right words in the right order.

I needed to get the word out to all JANSON clients and
our industry contacts about the tough bind that I was in, but I
also wanted to let them know that I was determined to continue
running and managing JANSON through this difficult situation

and that I was confident that, in time, we would make it through.

I wanted to let them know what was happening, but I also needed the tone to be upbeat, positive and forward looking. The takeaway I needed to convey was that I was still here, willing and able to do great work for my clients and fully committed to their goals and programs. After all, what we were experiencing wasn't unheard of in the business lifecycle. Every company, big and small, can expect to go through some unexpected market downturn, some financial catastrophe and some personnel crisis. JANSON just happened to be going through all of those things at the same time.

I could hear the writer scribbling furiously. "Got that?" I asked.

She answered in the affirmative, and in no time, she had a draft back to me. I made a few tweaks and sent it to my clients. How would they react? There was no telling.

I sat forward in my chair, folded my arms in front of me on the desk and put my head down. Why did everything have to come crashing down all at once? I brooded. It had been just a few days since the accountants had sprung this on me, though it felt like weeks at this point, and still I didn't have a plan. How was I going to figure this all out when I still was struggling to get my head around what it was exactly that had happened to me?

Raising my head, I looked across my desk at the various project files that needed attention. *Time to brace up*, I chided myself. I picked up the top folder and opened it. There was no point rehashing all my problems. It was time to get to work. The time flew, and by late that afternoon, many of my clients had emailed me or called. I was thrilled to find them understanding, supportive, even encouraging. In the wake of the September 11 Terrorist Attacks, just about every organization was struggling in some capacity. As with the rest of the country, they seemed to recognize that life and business "as usual" were being redefined and that we were all in it together.

It wasn't until Wednesday of the following week, though, that I heard from Renee, the marketing manager of our large account in California.

"I got a call from your employees," Renee stated abruptly the moment I put the receiver to my ear.

Here we go. I braced myself for bad news, gripping the top of the desk with my free hand. If this client opted to go...I shook my head and refused to catastrophize without real evidence.

"And..." I prodded, pushing her even further in my head. *Just say it already.*

"And the subject matter was quite strange," she stated.

I swallowed hard and tried to focus. She proceeded to give me a blow-by-blow account of the conversation. Apparently, my former employees were selling themselves pretty hard as an alternative to JANSON, and Renee had asked a lot of questions so she could take in the whole story.

Where would this end? I began waving my hand in frenetic circles, silently urging her to hurry up and get to the point.

Renee continued telling me how she kept pushing them until they were just spilling their guts about this new company they were starting and why her company needed to hire them. Then came a surprise, as she recounted exactly how she had wrapped up the conversation with them.

"'Okay, this all sounds good, but I'm confused: Where is Janet Chihocky in all of this?'"

Renee paused and then answered her own question: "'Because if Janet's still with JANSON, we're not leaving.'"

I slowly let out the breath I was holding when I heard her

give me an all-clear. "I just wanted to let you know, we're with you, Jan," she said. "I know it's tough but hang in there. You'll get through this."

I thanked her profusely, and when I placed the receiver down, I thanked God even more profusely. I felt in my heart that God was confirming for me once again to keep JANSON open. Over the next few days, more clients would call and let me know that they were sticking with me.

I didn't expect that and, to be honest, I didn't understand it. Why would they—or, for that matter, any other client—remain so loyal to JANSON, a tiny, five-year-old, now essentially one-person business, when there were so many other firms out there for the asking?

But then I remembered the promise of Revelation 3:8. "See, I have placed before you an open door that no one can shut."

The door was still open. Wide open. The question remained: Did I have enough faith and perseverance to walk all the way through it?

This wasn't the first time that I felt like God had intervened in JANSON's destiny and made a path forward. Two years prior and a little more than two years after Jeff and I had launched JANSON, our partnership had reached a crossroads that ultimately took us in separate directions.

At the time, we were doing more than well. It was the late 1990s, and the economy was in the midst of an ongoing boom, with no bust in site. New types of fast-maturing, cutting-edge technology, like e-mail, e-commerce, cell phones, satellite television and mobile tracking systems, had captured the imagination of both the consumer and the business world. Many people believed that we had reached the nirvana of a "New Economy," one in which services were replacing manufacturing as the economic engine and one in which business growth and market growth would continue in perpetuity. No longer, the thinking went, would we have to suffer through those pesky business cycles of expansion and recession. It would, of course, turn out to be an illusion.

For Jeff and me, however, starting a business in this environment made it all seem so easy. We were a two-person shop. We had a million-dollar contract with a multi-billion-dollar company. I was soon making regular trips to California to meet with our client's marketing staff, and our creative work was being seen in the premiere aviation and space industry trade media throughout the world.

Everything about the business, in the beginning, was fun and adventurous, and Jeff and I were both determined to establish ourselves as a legitimate, successful company. We were like two adolescent birds turned loose from the nest, and we were eager to show off how well we could fly.

In late 1998, we moved our desks and office supplies out of our respective homes and into 1,000 square feet of leased office space in Northern Virginia. We hired our first employees. One took care of back-office business tasks while another helped with production.

Jeff and I continued to work extremely well together. He was a great guy, a real salt-of-the-earth individual and a very talented creative director and designer. I was the face of the company, attending trade shows, networking with advertising salespeople and other industry contacts, making cold calls to potential customers, staying abreast of the space and aviation news occurring in the industries, constantly learning about the new technologies and the latest market entrants, making presentations and negotiating contracts. Neither of us was afraid of hard work. We loved what we did, and in due course, we were doing lucrative marketing work for other large aerospace players like Honeywell and Allied Signal, as well as a number of Tier 2 and Tier 3 firms.

What neither of us had, unfortunately, was a whole lot of operational knowledge or experience. We were all tactics, acting and reacting in the moment, responding to problems by seeking out advice from whoever happened to be nearby and taking that advice if it sounded good. I had written a business plan, but for us, it was just another box to be checked off, not something that we relied on to help drive our actions and eventual outcomes. We were good at making sales, creating ads and marketing collateral and supporting clients, but it didn't seem to dawn on us in those early days that we should be devoting just as much time to "the business."

Running a successful company, especially in a fast-changing, high-tech industry like aerospace, required so much more than the rudimentary, daily tasks of invoicing, accounting and filling out tax forms. We—or someone we hired—needed to devote study and energy to less tangible, everyday strategic activities like forecasting for growth, developing sales pipelines, managing cash flow and improving operational efficiency.

In short, there was a lot we didn't do because we didn't know we were supposed to be doing it.

We soon began figuring it out, but unfortunately, we learned the hard way.

Managing so much at once turned out to be a lot harder than I thought. It wasn't that I didn't know how to manage large ad expenditures or manage the client's expectations, it was that I'd never had to do it while also wearing about 10 other hats.

Another issue was cash flow. Accounts payable departments of large companies like to take their time when sending out payment for work already done. I hoped for 30-day terms so we could invoice on the first of the month and receive a check by the end, just in time to pay our regular expenses. On our end, the rent, phone and electric bill came due every month, and employees were paid every two weeks. Many companies, though, operated on 60-day terms and a few on 90-day terms.

This made for a gap between outgo and income, and soon we were building up debt.

I took it upon myself to find some way, any way, to get more cash flowing into our daily operation. Before we went full-time, Jeff and I had approached a bank about getting a $20,000 cash loan, but we were turned down. So I began to look around for a different type of workable solution, and before long, I heard about a local bank that was willing to "buy" our accounts receivable. They would give us the full amount of each invoice upfront and we'd have 90 days to pay them back. The cost? At the time, it didn't seem too high: just two percent interest on the amount "purchased." Certainly, it was better than a traditional loan or a credit card.

The debt, at that point, though, was manageable and would eventually be paid off as the company grew, or so I believed. We had made it over the first major hump of starting a new business, proving that there was a healthy demand for our particular brand of service, so why worry too much about carrying a little extra debt?

JANSON was steadily gaining new clients and increasing our gross revenues. We took that as a sign to loosen up and live a little, and both Jeff and I started spending some of our hard-earned money on personal items. To me, it seemed like a good time to "invest" in a new wardrobe that would help me "fit the part"; I soon found myself shopping all too frequently at the Ann Taylor Store at a nearby mall. And I probably spent too much time on the links, refining my golf game, which, I justified, was a necessary skill to have in the business world.

I even took time to travel. I had been praying for and supporting several missionaries who were working in Nairobi, Kenya, for some time, and in early 1999, on their invitation, I went to visit for a few weeks.

When I attended my first Sunday morning service at a church that had been planted by the missionaries, I was surprised to find that, although the sanctuary was filled with people, there were no cars in the parking lot. Everyone there had walked, some of them from miles away, for the chance to learn about and worship God. As I watched the African choir sing, I couldn't take my eyes off of one young woman. She sang the hymns with such passion and animation, and I could feel the Lord tugging on my heart to learn more about her. Kathy, my missionary friend, was more than happy to introduce us.

"This is Daisy Obdura," she told me afterward. I was surprised to find this youthful woman surrounded by children; two of them were clinging to her side and looking at me shyly. I shook Daisy's hand and told her how much I enjoyed listening to her beautiful voice. She flashed the brightest smile at me, but I soon learned that it hid a tragic past. Like many people in her village and the surrounding region, her husband had died of AIDS, leaving her behind to raise seven children on her own. "It has been difficult," she admitted in a soft voice. "But God has been so faithful to me. Every day he makes sure we have what we need."

She had such strength and faith, but I felt deep in my heart that God had brought me there to help her and make sure that she continued to get whatever she and her family needed. With Kathy's help, I began sponsoring the children so they could attend a local school full-time. I sent cash each month to help Daisy feed, house and clothe her family. And for the children, I would lovingly fill and ship care-packages of toys, snacks and extra clothes.

They were all so grateful, and Daisy wrote me often to remind me how much it was helping. "We thank you for remembering us," she wrote in one letter soon after my trip. "We are very proud. We hope our friendship will continue forever." And in another one: "May God bless the work of your hands and greet all your friends from the JANSON company....P.S. We love you."

They were such a blessing to me! Getting their letters each month provided perspective on the smallness of my own problems, and it was humbling to see their faith in action. I resolved to continue to support the Obdura family for as long as they needed me.

As the new Millennium approached, JANSON was still growing, the clients were happy and Jeff and I were getting along great. But I soon began noticing a weakness in our business model that grew slowly into a more obvious crack. Initially, I couldn't quite put my finger on it, but something was wrong, and it nagged at me.

We both worked hard, but as I continued studying the fast-changing market, I began to realize that the company and its services needed to evolve with it. I became more aggressive in my stance on that. In my mind, if we were going to survive for the long haul, we needed to progress from a creative shop into a firm that focused more on strategy. To do that, I would need to strengthen my own skills, to become more strategic in nature and less tactical.

Marketing communications was an element in the value stream, but it was too far down the stream. To be a more formidable player, JANSON needed to provide more value by working more closely with clients. And for that to happen, we needed a shift in operation—a big one.

In this new role, we wouldn't just come in on the back-end to create marketing collateral or advertising campaigns to the client's specifications. We would be a partner in actually determining those specifications based on the client's growth and priorities. We would be a trusted adviser on the most core aspects of their business, from launching new products and services to providing the research and analysis needed to improve decision-making and strengthen their competitive position to overseeing communications with all stakeholders, including the media.

To be a strategically minded firm would make us a lot more, in the trade parlance, "sticky." We would be so valuable, so vital to the client's business that they would see us more like a partner than a transaction-based service.

There was a part of me that wanted to remain exactly as we were: a boutique creative agency that produced high-quality, impressive marketing products. It was important, and a part of what I wanted for the business, but it was also, essentially, a commodity. Niche agencies were everywhere, and new ones were popping up all the time. Could this business model sustain us for the long-term? Was it enough of a discriminator?

It became increasingly clear that we needed to be something more significant to our clients—both for their sake and for ours.

The more we contemplated this, the more I began to feel that maybe a partnership, or at least this partnership, didn't serve JANSON's best interests and wouldn't get us to where I felt we needed to go.

I began to have a thought, first occasionally and then over and over: Maybe it was time to go it alone.

As had become my pattern; I began to pray in earnest for guidance. Whatever route I took, I needed God to lead me. I wanted to know and follow God's will.

But I was torn. There was no better man than Jeff. He was so kind and so supportive. And he had been with me from the beginning of this journey and walked every step with me, without conflict, without complaining. Was I doing the right thing? Even thinking about ending the partnership was painful. Was that a sign that I was off track? Maybe this was all me, insisting on my will, not God's. Was I being arrogant? Greedy? I was part of a successful, growing business—wasn't that enough?

Over time, the more I prayed, the more I felt sure that God was leading me in these thoughts, that it was the right decision, the right path forward. I felt peace about it, felt it in my spirit.

When I finally approached Jeff, however, it was still exceptionally difficult. We talked for a long time and after much discussion, we mutually agreed that, while what we'd managed to build together was really great, it was time for our season together as partners to come to an end. Jeff agreed that he would sell me his share.

Just to make everything fair, we hired an outside CPA to conduct the financial due diligence and formulate a buy-out price. We went to her office on a Wednesday morning after she'd spend some time tabulating our assets, including our existing contracts, and our liabilities. She also took into account the fact that company was just a few years old. She then gave her verdict: The entire business was worth $100,000. After conferring with Jeff, the CPA suggested that he could hold the loan of $49,000, his share of the valuation, and I could pay him with interest over time, or if I came up with the cash right now, he'd accept a flat sales price of $35,000 for his 49 percent stake.

Jeff indicated that he preferred the latter deal. I tried not to give away my position, but inwardly, I was nodding my head enthusiastically in agreement.

"Well, what do you say?" the accountant prodded. "Do you have the $35,000 to buy him out right now, or should we go ahead and start negotiating some mutually agreeable terms?

I didn't answer her right away. A one-and-done deal would free both of us to move forward immediately in our respective lives, but the money I brought to the table had to be personal. And all I had at the moment was $5,000 in savings.

"Well?" she asked again.

"I have a few thousand," I mumbled honestly. "Let me work on it."

The accountant suggested that we give it a few days and meet back in her office on Monday. If I could come up with the money, we could finalize the buyout then, and if not, Jeff and I could work out the loan terms.

I owned 51 percent of the business and now God had given me a golden opportunity to acquire the other 49 percent, but "the how" required to get from here to there seemed impossible. JANSON itself had been turned down for a $20,000 loan not that long ago, so the odds of a bank offering even more money on my own personal merits didn't seem promising.

I started to think through some options: Home equity loan? I wasn't sure I had enough to tap. Cash advance on a couple of credit cards? I was sure that probably wasn't a good idea.

Once again, I hit my knees and prayed. "God, I feel like you have led me to make this shift," I told Him. "If this is Your will and not mine, please direct me to where I can secure these funds. Show me what to do."

Thursday came and went with no answer and so did Friday. After work, I went to my mother's house for a visit. We walked outside to her front porch, drank some tea and talked more about the situation. I had run out of funding ideas and was now thinking about the kind of loan terms I'd be able to realistically afford. I listed them out to Mom and began ruminating on the chances that Jeff would accept them.

Then Mom's phone rang.

"Roger!" my mother answered brightly after pushing the talk button on her cordless phone. "How are you?"

She placed a hand over the receiver and whispered in my direction, "It's Roger Parsons," before continuing with the phone conversation. I could hear him asking her about her church group, and in her usual animated way, she proceeded to give him lots of details about their current activities and upcoming plans.

Roger and his wife, Millie, had long been members of our church. Roger himself was a retired Army colonel and carried himself with the regal bearing that came from living the structured, disciplined Army life for most of his adult life. Nonetheless, he never intimidated anyone. He was completely approachable, steadfast in his faith, a genuinely kind and happy man who always had the sweetest smile on his face, even after his wife passed away.

Over the previous two years, he'd taken an interest in JANSON and always made it a point to ask me how the business was going. His inquiries were never rhetorical. He posed well-thought-out questions about my clients and current and upcoming projects, and always followed up my answers with more questions. I'm not sure why he was so interested, though it was probably the dichotomy of my situation. Let's be honest: How many 29-year-old women could be found talking after church about satellite constellations and space launch vehicles? Thinking about it now, it was probably quite intriguing to a former military man, but whatever the reason, I always enjoyed talking with him. He became a kind of well-seasoned mentor to me, someone who served as a safe sounding board for my ideas and business concerns. I could always count on him to provide honest and sound, faith-based advice.

Mom was still talking about the church when she suddenly changed the subject: "You know, Jan is here visiting me."

She listened for a moment and then handed me the phone. "He wants to talk to you," she said.

I wasn't surprised when the conversation immediately began with: "So how are things with you, Jan? How is JANSON?"

Determined to remain upbeat, I gave him a status report of some of our more interesting projects, but I had no desire to discuss the conundrum in which I currently found myself.

Roger kept prodding me to be more specific, and I continued listing out all the good things that were happening with the business.

The phone went quiet for a moment, but then Roger said, "You know, Jan, I feel like you're holding something back. Are you sure there is nothing else going on in your business that you want to talk about?"

I was taken aback by his bluntness, but since I knew that he was genuine in his concern, I decided to be forthcoming. "Well, Roger, my business partner and I have mutually decided to part ways and I have an opportunity to buy out his shares," I explained. "Jeff's a good man, but I believe in my spirit that JANSON needs to go in a slightly different direction. I want to make sure this is only done on good terms."

I didn't provide any details about the accountant or the agreed-upon terms for how much I needed to bring to the table, but I expected Roger to chime in with his usual follow-up questions. He didn't. In fact, he remained quiet for a few moments. Finally, he said, "Jan, I feel like I should help you. God has really had you on my heart of late. I am not sure how much you need to come up with to buy out your partner, but will $15,000 help?"

Help?! Are you kidding me? That would provide exactly half of the $30,000 I needed. It was more help than I could ever expect.

"Yes, of course," I answered him, before breaking down into tears right there on the phone.

"How soon do you need the money," he asked.

"Very soon," I managed to get out.

"Let me work out some details. I'll call you tomorrow to let you know where you can pick up a check," Roger said. I heard him chuckle as he could obviously detect my joy even as I thanked him repeatedly through sobs and sniffles.

I hung up and ran into the house to look for my mother, who had gone in to let me talk in private. I was still crying.

"He's offered to loan me $15,000!" I shouted when I found her. "Can you believe it?"

She clasped her hands together, but the look on her face showed me she did believe. "Praise the Lord, Jan," she said. "He always answers prayers."

The next morning, Roger called. I didn't even wait to see his number on the caller ID before I grabbed it and pushed the talk button.

Even as I was saying hello, I was reaching into my kitchen drawer and pulling out a pen and small notebook, so I could jot down the address of the bank branch he was calling about. After a couple of pleasantries, though, he didn't offer those details. Instead, he said, "Jan, I have to tell you: I was really restless last night. I just sensed the Lord was speaking to me about this particular situation."

I held my breath. It had been an awfully generous offer, but it was also spur of the moment. *Had he changed his mind?* I thought I might turn completely blue as I waited for him to continue.

"I really feel led to help you with another $15,000, so that would be a total of $30,000," he explained. "Would that be enough?"

What?! Did he say $30,000? Did I hear right? I had $5,000 in hand, but I needed another $30,000. How did he know? I had never given him a specific figure, never told him how much I needed. Clearly, this was a God thing.

I again failed at holding back the tears as Roger told me he was contacting his bank and would FedEx me a cashier's check for arrival at JANSON's offices on Monday morning.

Sure enough, the FedEx truck rolled in before 10 a.m. I quickly signed for it, snatched the envelope and raced to the bank to deposit it in my personal account. When I walked into the accountant's office for our 1 p.m. meeting, I handed the accountant a check written out to Jeff for the exact amount: $35,000.

The accountant looked at the check and then looked at me. She seemed bewildered. "I thought you needed a loan," she said. "How in the world did you get this?"

"Prayer," I stated simply.

"Well, I don't know what God you believe in, but He must be real," she said. She handed the check to Jeff, who was also surprised to see that he'd been paid in full.

I put a hand on Jeff's arm, wished him well and thanked him. I could never forget him, the friend and supportive business partner he had been to me. I may have been the "JAN" but he was the "SON" and together we had created JANSON.

As I hung up with Renee that morning, I felt ecstatic. My big client, JANSON's first major account, was going to stick with me! I continued to thank God in my head, even as I raced away from my desk, once again searching for my mother so I could share my news.

"Mom!" I yelled as I jerked my office door open. She was sitting at the receptionist's desk as usual, but she spun around immediately to face me. "God's got His hand on us! He's going to protect us. They're all staying!"

She clasped her hands together and looked up again. This time she didn't say anything. She had known what was at stake, and when she looked back down and at me, there were tears streaming down her face. I didn't have to ask, for I knew what she was thinking. *God will make a way.*

Even though I still had all my clients, I would have to start over again in a way. All of the behaviors and criteria I had seen as "normal" for me, that were familiar, would have to be challenged. Now I had to figure out what my "new normal" would look like. I knew it would be hard because I still didn't trust myself, still didn't know if I could make a good decision. But starting from a largely blank slate could also be liberating, a chance to rewrite my past, to right all the wrongs I'd done.

As I cheerfully ambled to my office and went back to work that day, I was hopeful for the future. *Everything will be okay,* I thought happily. I put aside any thoughts about the mountain of debt I still had to contend with, the employees that were no longer there to help me, the uncertain, anemic marketplace.

I didn't care what was next, just that I was pointed upward, though anyone looking in from the outside would likely believe that my wings had been clipped and that I had done it to myself.

Maybe so, but I was sure in that moment that I wouldn't be grounded for long. *God will make a way.* That's what I had heard my whole life at home and in church. And I believed it. I knew He would come through, somehow, someway.

But when? It had been over a week now. By the next day, true to form, I was already starting to grow impatient with the wait.

SIX

WHERE IS THAT
FEDEX TRUCK?

But if we hope for what we do not see, we eagerly wait for it with perseverance. Romans 8:25

The next morning, I sat down at my desk and breathed out a huge sigh of relief. My most prestigious client was sticking around. JANSON still had ongoing, paying work, work that I was sure would grow and bring in more revenues once the market righted itself and started to come back.

All signs pointed in the direction that I felt God was leading me, and in my heart, I was beginning to believe that I could actually handle this. What I needed now was a plan and an action list of how to get from here to there. I was both nervous and excited to get started—nervous over how bad the bleed may be and excited to move a step forward.

As I headed out to the reception area to grab a cup of coffee, Jeanne, my good friend from church, walked into the office. She'd been there with me that first night at church when the pastor and church elders had encircled me and prayed for me.

Since then, she'd called just about every night, just to check in.

Now she wanted to do more. "You know what you need around here?" she asked, putting her hands on her hips and looking around the offices. "A new paint job, a way to wash away the old and bring in the new."

"You want to paint my office?" I asked, a bit incredulous.

"I do. What do you say?"

"Well, I can't afford much, but I guess I can afford a can or two of paint," I laughed.

After Jeanne headed out, promising to come back in a couple of days, I poured my cup of coffee and sat down at my desk.

First up? Get back to paying work. Now that I knew that business would go on—although certainly not at the clip we had been at before 9/11—I needed to finish offloading our ongoing projects to outside consultants. We had long relied on a stable of reliable freelancers to handle a lot of the tasks, like concepting, copywriting, proofreading, designing. Unlike regular employees, freelancers didn't have any taxes withheld from their checks nor were they entitled to benefits. As such, I didn't have to pay the extra payroll tax on what they earned or carry a portion of their premiums on our health insurance plan. That made it a clean transaction and easy to budget for, unlike full-time employees, who I had to continue to pay no matter how much actual paying work we had at any given time.

I picked up the phone and started making calls. With each consultant, I discussed the pertinent details of each assignment and the schedule. As each project was completed, I could submit invoices to the client and simultaneously send a copy over to the bank, which purchased the invoices, minus their two percent fee. This would inject immediate cash into JANSON's coffers.

The majority of the consultants were more than happy to

take on the extra work and eager to get started. One consultant, though, snapped me back to reality. Her most recent invoice, she explained, hadn't been paid as yet. Did I know when a check was being sent?

Oops! There was no need to panic. Apologizing profusely, I promised to look into it and take care of it as soon as possible.

As I hung up the phone with the freelancer, the responsibility suddenly draped over me like a sopping wet blanket. I got up from my chair and walked out of my office to spend some time with my mother and get some encouragement. I found her organizing and reorganizing our files in between answering the phone. She looked up when she saw me coming, the head-hanging walk from my desk to hers a clear physical communication that I was in need of one of her famous pep talks.

I knew it was time to stop putting off the inevitable. I needed to take full stock of JANSON's financial situation, but I was afraid of what I would find. As I approached, Mom gave me a reassuring smile and answered before I even had a chance to ask the question. "Jan, I know this is hard for you, but you hang in there and take it one step at a time."

It wasn't profound, just another take on her favorite saying— *"Brace up"*—but it gave me a boost and helped me get over my mental hurdle and move forward. I nodded, and as I turned to walk back into my office, I could hear her murmuring a prayer. I don't know how she did it, but Mom always seemed to know when I needed a ton of advice and when it was more appropriate to take it straight to God and intercede on my behalf.

I sat down, pulled my chair close to my desk and spread out the collection of files sent over from the accountant's office, including a packet of unpaid bills. Then I pulled out a legal pad, drawing a vertical line down the middle to delineate two columns: one for money that was due now and the other listing the total amount of debt owed to each creditor. In between pen taps, I jotted down all the numbers.

It wasn't a pretty picture by any stretch of the imagination. By the time I tallied everything up late that afternoon, I was ready to jump out of my chair and bolt through the door. To steady myself, I hooked my feet around the chair legs and leaned backwards as if reality would somehow look better from a distance.

The debts were numerous and, in some cases, enormous. We were behind on the rent, the phone and the electric. There were outstanding invoices from freelancers for work they'd done months prior. Ads that we had placed for clients—and which had already run in trade publications—had not yet been paid; staring back at me from the invoices were angry declarations in red ink, "Payment is PAST DUE," and even angrier demands, stamped in a larger typeface, to "PAY NOW."

Several corporate credit cards were near their charging limit, as was the line of credit. These, along with the "factoring" arrangement I had with the bank to "buy" my client invoices upfront, were all weapons in the arsenal I'd stockpiled to help combat my ongoing cash flow problems. All of these bills, too, were either past due or nearing their due date.

One statement stood out for me: the next payment due to the bank that provided me with advances against my client invoices. The bill wasn't overdue yet, but when I looked at the complex list of advances paid out and then the equally complex list of payback amounts and due dates, I could feel my heart begin to race. The next payment was due within a week. The amount? Nearly $20,000. But the cash I needed to pay it wasn't in my bank account, and I couldn't make it be there.

What had seemed like an acceptable solution with the bank buying our invoices had quickly transformed into the proverbial house of cards that was now teetering and in danger of total collapse.

Shaking off the thought, I forced myself to focus on completing the main task on my action list. I pulled out a calculator, punched in all of the various debt numbers listed out on my legal pad and then punched them in one more time just to be sure. I leaned even further back in my chair and rubbed my eyes to hold back the tears that threatened to erupt.

The grand total? Nearly half a million dollars.

"This can't be!" I exclaimed, much louder than I intended. I could feel my emotions swimming rapidly towards the surface. To ward them off, I got up, stretched my arms behind me to loosen my upper back muscles and started pacing around the office. How in the world had it gotten to be this bad? Half a million dollars might not sound like very much to a lot of companies, but it is when it accounts for more than a third of your total annual revenues. I plopped back down in my chair. Why hadn't the accountants said anything to me before they suggested that I file for bankruptcy?

For the first time, I wondered: Had they been telling me, and I just hadn't listened? Was I suffering from some form of denial? Looking back, I realized that the accountants had probably been whispering their concerns to me. But if the boat is sinking, a whisper isn't going to cut it. You need someone who isn't afraid to make some noise, shouting out loud so there's no chance for misunderstanding: *Start bailing NOW!*

The process they set up was pretty cut-and-dried. I would do a cursory review of all the invoices and bills before sending them over to be paid, so it was possible that they thought I knew what was going on. But didn't they have at least a moral obligation to shout or at least warn, *Hey! You're getting pretty close to your limits, so you might want to quit spending so much, start cutting expenses or maybe pick up on the work...and fast?*

If only they'd cared enough about me, about the business, to raise the volume and try to get my attention. But would I have listened then? I couldn't say.

At this point, it didn't matter. This debt was my pitfall, my responsibility. I had chosen to align with a firm that viewed their role as purely transactional, rather than as a relational or advisory one.

I heard the phone ringing again. When it stopped, I could tell by the louder and higher-pitched tone of my mother's voice wafting through the door that it was likely a creditor calling about a late payment.

As much as I wanted to run from the call, I took it. The woman, from a local vendor, politely explained that they had not yet received last month's payment. Was I aware?

"Yes, I understand that we need to make that payment," I explained. "But we're going through some challenging times right now."

The voice on the other end seemed a bit thrown by my answer, and she stumbled a bit as if looking for the appropriate response somewhere in her script.

"Yes, um, okay. But will you be able to send out a check today?

"No, I can't," I replied honestly. "But we will get it to you as soon as we can."

She ended by reminding me that if I didn't respond by a certain date, they'd have to cut off my credit and turn the account over to a collections agency.

I hung up the phone and gritted my teeth. *Brace up*, I ordered. There was no use spending time or energy on self-pity. I studied again the columns of numbers lined up next to each other and the total amount at the bottom of the page.

I reached into my desk and grabbed a red pen, jotted a dollar sign next to the massive figure and circled it several times.

This was what I had to deal with. How I had gotten here didn't matter, at least not anymore. This was my business, my fault, my problem. I had no one to blame but myself.

Ironically, in the first 18 months after I'd taken JANSON solo, the business had soared. Our client base had expanded to more than a dozen well-established commercial companies, along with numerous smaller but up-and-coming firms.

They provided steady business and, to keep up, I began hiring the best employees I could afford: in-house designers, production staff and account managers.

Eager to continue growing the company, I spent a great deal of my time on the road, attending trade shows, networking with business prospects and meeting with clients. The work we were doing was top-notch and word about it was starting to spread, which made my sales efforts a lot easier. I found that people were more than willing to take my calls and sit in on presentations, and some companies had even started seeking me out. By the late summer of 2001, our revenues were growing at a strong clip.

My operational problems, unfortunately, didn't disappear with all the new activity. In fact, they got more complicated. For starters, the new staff members were expensive. I had hired them and calculated their salaries on a simple equation: JANSON would gain a revenue return equal to anywhere from two to two-and-a-half times the amount of each salary. For larger projects, that was definitely the case, but unfortunately, the bigger deals had not yet become the norm. Most of our projects continued to be small- to mid-paying jobs.

As a result, depending on the month, JANSON wasn't always earning enough to completely offset the sizable salaries, a fact that meant I was slowly but steadily adding more to JANSON's debt load. I had made a mistake that wasn't uncommon in small businesses: I had over-hired.

It didn't dawn on me to start making cuts. Why would it? As far as I could see, the company was doing fine. We were continually adding a new client here and there and we stayed plenty busy with the projects that we did have.

Plus, by then, I had managed to open a corporate line of credit, though I had to secure it personally with the equity I had in my home. The decision was risky, yes, but the open line gave me a way to smooth out the occasional bump that popped up along my financial journey each month. Wasn't there such a concept as good debt, a transitory condition that, like weight, went up and down over time?

I predicted nothing but good times ahead, though my conclusions were based solely on my optimistic observations and hopes. There was no urge to tap the brakes and gain control before heading into the next turn. Rather, I pushed down on the accelerator. That August, JANSON signed a long-term lease on the offices across the hall. We'd be hiring additional employees fairly soon, I reasoned, and we would need the extra space.

Even in the days after the September 11 Terrorist Attacks, I wasn't concerned about the future of the business. We were all shocked, of course, and grief-stricken by all the televised images of destruction and death. The news was coming in fast. Within the hour, friends who worked closer to Washington, D.C., were calling to tell me that they could actually see black smoke rising up from the Pentagon, which had taken its own direct hit after the first two planes flew into the World Trade Center Towers in New York. And though we didn't know anyone personally who had been killed, we had friends and business colleagues who did.

Still, work at JANSON continued on without any major interruption, and I remained optimistic. Until early November, that is.

At that point, the events and uncertainty that were still dominating the country's psyche finally caught up to the business cycle. Subtly at first but then more obviously, JANSON clients started pulling back on projects. Some told me they needed to downsize upcoming projects. Others wanted to put off the start of a new campaign until after the New Year. A few client prospects that had verbally committed to a relationship never called back.

By the middle of the month, I realized that the workload was down by nearly half. I wasn't panicked, though, still believing this was a temporary slowdown. I intensified my sales efforts, focused my employees on completing the work projects that we did have in the queue and cheered myself with the thought that once the holidays passed client spending would pick back up again.

It didn't. And so here I sat. No employees other than my mother. Very little cash. Not much credit. And a mountain of debt. I took another deep breath, gathered all the bills and filed them away.

After taking another sip of what was now lukewarm coffee, I opened up the QuickBooks financial application on my computer. There at the bottom of the screen was my income and expense statement for the last four months, a simple graph that told the story of my company's sudden collapse in simple red and green lines. The expenses had remained largely the same, while the revenues had plunged southward.

I looked at the figure on the legal pad, circled ominously in red: $500,000. It was time to find places to cut costs—and fast.

I heard the door open. "Jan," my mother called softly. "I'm going to head on home and get some dinner. Can I get you anything?"

Looking up, I saw that the sky had already turned dark. It was after 5 p.m. "No, I'm okay," I told her, giving her a half-smile. "Don't worry. I'll call you later."

As the door closed behind her, I stood up and walked around the office, shaking my arms and legs as if to threaten away any negative feelings that might try to reach out and pull me down. I flipped the page on the legal pad and, referencing the checkbook register in the QuickBooks file, started writing down the list of JANSON's monthly, recurring expenses.

Some expenses were being slowly eliminated by attrition, most notably payroll. Once I cut a final check to all of my now ex-employees, JANSON's monthly outgo would drop significantly. Not only did I no longer have to cover their hefty salaries, but I would also save on payroll taxes, health insurance premiums and other added benefits.

Other expenses would also drop simply by not having all those extra employees on site, including electric, water and phone.

Besides these, I couldn't identify much that could be cut. We were locked into a long-term lease, including the new office space. A lot of our monthly outgo went to the interest on the debt. And my mother's salary was sacrosanct. She was a big help around the office, and besides, she desperately needed the relatively small paycheck she got every two weeks.

I kept going down the register on the screen. One entry jumped out at me: *Janet Chihocky*. It was written to cover my own pay for the past two weeks. There was no doubt I made a healthy annual income. In better times, it was hardly exorbitant, right in line with what a CEO of a small marketing company in the Washington, D.C., region would expect to make. But now? JANSON could no longer afford me.

I wrote down my salary and then immediately slashed through the figure with my red pen. I would no longer pay myself a dime. That would definitely free up some cash for JANSON.

How would I pay for my mortgage, my car loan, my food and other basic needs? I'd have to get by on my personal savings for a while. Fortunately, I'd been much more fiscally conservative in my own personal finances in the two years since I'd drained my savings to buy out Jeff, earmarking a healthy percentage of my salary for my rainy-day fund. That rainy day had arrived.

My fortunes would only rise again if, and when, JANSON's did.

The next morning, I arrived early but found myself unable to concentrate. I had wanted to spend at least an hour before the office officially opened doing normal JANSON work: answering client emails, looking over some of the ad copy that a freelance writer had submitted overnight and preparing invoices. Within minutes of sitting down at my desk, the phone was already ringing.

"Good morning. JANSON Communications," I answered, doing my best to sound bright and business-as-usual.

It was yet another creditor. *Blast it!*

I fell back on the same basic script I had used the day before. "We are working through a challenging season," I told the voice on the other end of the line. "We do not have the funds to pay you today, but as soon as we have the funds, we will send the overdue payment."

"Well, thank you for your honesty," the voice replied. "We will check in with you again next week."

"I doubt the situation will have changed by then," I said frankly as I ended the call.

I hung up the phone and felt deflated. I tapped my pen, jumped up and walked purposefully over to the window.

Where is that FedEx truck? I thought impatiently. It had been part of God's previous answer when I needed money. Surely, it would come again one of these days, bringing with it a big, fat check that would miraculously solve all of my problems.

Letting out an irritated sigh, I pressed my head against the glass and closed my eyes. I asked for providence. *"Please, God, I know you've got a plan, a solution to all this. But please bring it soon.*

The phone was ringing again when Mom showed up. Before she picked it up, I asked her to just take a message, explaining that I'd get back to whoever was on the other end. "I don't want to deal with any of it for a little while," I told her. Then, breathing a sigh of relief, I shut my door, put the phone ringer on quiet and tried to get some work done. I spent the next couple of hours talking to clients and consultants, answering emails and updating invoices.

Through the walls, though, I could hear the phone ringing and couldn't help worrying which of them were creditors. I tried to shut out the thoughts if only to shut down my anxiety.

The mailman came later that morning, and when I realized it, I rushed out to the reception area. Mom usually sorted the mail, but I pushed past her and began to frantically rifle through the envelopes, automatically translating the contents by the name listed in the left-hand corner. Bill. Bill. Direct mail flyer about an upcoming trade show. Another bill. No checks.

Ugh! I had to make a $19,600 payment to the bank in less than a week. I started pacing around the reception area, clenching my fists open and shut. I cast a glance at my mother, who quickly turned back to her computer as if she was afraid she might be the unwitting target of a sudden verbal outburst. I tried to relax and managed a weak smile in her direction.

"I'm going for a walk," I told her as gently as possible.

I stepped across the hall and started touring through the brand-new office space that we'd leased and furnished and never used. I couldn't help noting for the first time just how much stuff we had: L-shaped computer workstations, hutches, supply cabinets, lamps, credenzas that doubled as printer stands. I had wasted so much money prepping for the clients and employees I had imagined were coming but who had never arrived.

We didn't need at least half of the office furniture and equipment we had anymore. That was obvious. And we'd probably never need it. I walked back to the receptionist area and got my mother's attention.

"Hey, can you get in touch with one of the local office discount stores and see if they're buying office furniture right now, and if so, how much they're paying?"

She jerked her head up and looked at me, her eyes starting to water up. "No, no," I replied, softening my voice and putting a hand on her shoulder. "I'm not giving up. We just need to raise some cash—and quick."

She nodded and squeezed my hand. Then she pulled out the Yellow Pages, flipped through until she located the needed number and made the call.

I looked around inside some of the other offices and cubicles in the space beyond the reception area. There was other equipment that we might be able to offload as well, like computers, printers, an extra copy machine. We'd get a pittance in exchange, but it was something, and there was no point putting it off.

I heard her ask my questions to the person on the other end and then, "Can you hold on for a moment?"

She gestured for me to take the call. "They're buying," she said, handing me the receiver. "They're paying 40 percent of the value, and they'll come pick it up if you want."

I nodded. "It will be okay, Mom," I told her, my words of reassurance meant as much for me as for her. Then I took the receiver. "Yes," I said. "When could you come out?"

Tuesday was almost a mirror of Monday. Creditors started calling early. No checks came in the mail. I worked from early in the morning until late in the evening. And another friend, Melinda, who was also my mother's neighbor, showed up without notice but ready to provide whatever support we needed.

Melinda had "personality plus," as we like to say in the South, injecting an energy and a sass to our serious little crisis that made it a lot easier for me to keep a smile on my face. As a former fashion buyer for Saks 5th Avenue, she was always dressed to the nines, as if she were ready to head up to the Hamptons for the weekend.

"What can I do?" she asked.

The phone started ringing before I could answer. I glanced at the caller ID and joked, "Want to deal with the creditors?"

"Let me at 'em," she replied with a grin. "Sounds like fun."

I handed her the list of creditors that needed to be called. She started dialing the numbers and bluntly told them that we were aware of the situation and that we'd be in touch. "I know you have your job to do," she said sweetly. "But give us a break, okay? We'll be in touch as soon as we can."

On Wednesday and Thursday, Jeanne showed up with her buckets of paint and went to work, humming cheerfully as she rolled two fresh coats of a neutral tone on the walls of the reception area. Mom moved into another office, opening up all the windows for ventilation, and she and I kept working despite the rancid smell. When Jeanne finished and cleaned up at the end of each day, she would come into my office and pray with me. She had picked up on my growing feelings of impatience and despair, despite my best efforts to keep smiling.

"God's in control," she told me on Thursday evening, making it a point to write down a couple of encouraging Biblical verses that I should read that night before bed. "Remember, His solution won't look anything like what you think it's supposed to look like."

By Friday morning, another cursory flip through the morning's mail made it obvious that the client check was not coming. My payment to the bank was now officially overdue. Mom knocked on my door early that afternoon. "It's the bank," she said. "They want to talk to you."

I picked up the phone, and before the loan officer on the other end could even say why she was calling, I was apologizing.

"I've got a cash flow crisis going on, and I do not yet have the funds here to make the payment," I explained. "I need more time."

She knew me and was sympathetic. "We can give you a 10-day grace period," she stated.

Grace. It was ironic how that word had been appropriated by the credit industry. I couldn't help thinking of Jesus at that moment. "My grace is sufficient for thee," Jesus had told the

Apostle Paul, "for my strength is made perfect in weakness."

I slumped forward in prayer. "Here's your chance, God, to show your strength," I said out loud. "I don't see how I can get any weaker."

It was late in the afternoon and my mom headed home. My Uncle Warren was coming in from Tennessee that evening, and she still hadn't had a chance to grocery shop or prepare the spare bedroom. He was her oldest living brother, and as with all of my uncles, I looked forward to seeing him. I just loved being around my mom's siblings.

"Don't work too late," she admonished me. "And plan to come over tomorrow. We'll have dinner about six."

She hugged me. "Don't lose faith," she said. "Just keep praying. Hold in there."

The next evening, I relaxed over dinner, as Uncle Warren regaled us with all the latest happenings in southeastern Tennessee. I loved to hear him and Mom banter back and forth about some of their favorite memories growing up in their quiet little hometown. I just loved Uncle Warren. He was such a kind man, much more introverted than my mother, but full of life and joy. I had always had a special relationship with him and his daughter Becky, despite the fact that she was 20 years older than me.

While we were clearing the plates afterward, he piped up. "Hey, Jan, why don't you take me sightseeing in Washington tomorrow?"

I brightened. Though I was a bit surprised at the suggestion, I jumped at the chance. This excursion would be a good distraction, a chance to spend some quality time with my uncle and relax a bit. "Sure thing. What time?"

That night after Mom walked me to my car, I asked if she thought I should ask Uncle Warren for some help. He was hardly wealthy, but he was "comfortable," as my mother liked to say euphemistically. I'd never asked him for money before and I felt funny even considering it now. Would he think less of me? I didn't want this to affect my relationship with him.

"Pray about it," Mom told me. "And if you feel led to ask him, go ahead and ask."

The next morning, we all went to church, and afterward, Uncle Warren climbed down into the passenger seat of my little car, hanging onto the sides of the seat as I zipped through traffic and headed into the city. It was a beautiful day, cool but sunny, and we had a wonderful time.

We toured the Washington National Cathedral and then drove back for a leisurely stroll around the National Mall and its various monuments. As we walked, he asked me questions about JANSON and I, in turn, asked him about Becky, my cousin. She was a generation ahead of me, so I didn't know her much growing up, but as I had aged, she became a friend and a steady-state cousin I could count on for support and compassion. I just found it easy to talk with her, and she was so proud of me and what I had accomplished.

"She's doing great," he said. "Such a wonderful girl."

Uncle Warren and Becky had a close relationship, and he beamed when he talked about the blessing she had been since his wife (Becky's mom and my aunt) had passed away. Becky was always calling, stopping by for long chats and making sure he had everything he needed.

After a while, we sat down on a bench, and I felt like I needed to confide my situation. He listened carefully with great concern.

Then, without any prodding from me, he asked: "How much do you need right now?"

"Anything you want to loan me would be great, Uncle, but please let the amount be something decided between you and God."

Uncle Warren nodded and then leaned forward towards the ground, his hands locked. To me, this wasn't about brokering a deal or solving a problem on my terms. I wanted to surrender this all to God, to plant a seed and just "wait." That was the hardest part, but whatever the outcome I could easily point to God and say: "Look at what He did!"

We sat quietly for a long while. A flock of pigeons caught the corner of my eye as they circled low over the nearby cascade of waterfalls and granite walls and then floated down softly on the sidewalk in front of us.

Uncle Warren watched them as well before straightening back up and turning towards me. "You know, I'll have to run this by Becky first, but would $20,000 help?"

It would more than help.

"Yes, absolutely," I said, smiling and moving in for a hug. "That would be perfect."

A sense of peace came over me. I was certain that Becky would agree to the loan, not because she was flippant about money, but because she had such a good heart and, like Uncle Warren, would want to help me if at all possible.

And sure enough, on Monday morning, Becky called. "I'm putting the check in the mail today," she said.

Ironically, it was later that night when a deep despair suddenly set in on me and dark thoughts began to take over. Yes, Uncle Warren's willingness to help had been a Godsend, but once again, I had succeeded in simply paying off one loan by taking out another, and this time it was family that I might end up leaving on the hook.

As I climbed into bed that night, a spirit of fear came over me. *You're going to lose everything!* Voices of doubt began screaming at me. *Why are you even trying? You can't do this!* Feelings of terror began to take over, and I started to tremble. I tried desperately to push the thoughts away, but they kept coming back.

I was so exhausted, both physically and emotionally, and that's because no matter how much support I had from my family and friends, I was the one bearing the weight. I was the one walking through the wilderness. It was all on me, and I didn't want to carry this load, I didn't want to walk this journey any longer. The guilt, shame and loneliness slammed into me like a series of rogue waves and my mind was suddenly flooded with cruel accusations: *You don't have enough work to stay afloat— and you never will! You're not qualified! You failed once, and you'll just keep on failing!*

And with that, I slipped down into a lower level of the pit, this one so deep and so dark that I began to genuinely believe that there was no way out. I thought about losing everything and wondered how hard, how humiliating it would be to start over. I feared that I would never be able to pay off the debtors. At this point, I was probably worth more dead than I was alive. I was consumed with doubt, doubt in myself and doubt that I was capable of even making a good decision. Just starting JANSON had been a mistake, I admitted to myself. I was in a role I wasn't fit for and couldn't succeed at. I tried on the shame of being viewed as a loser, a deadbeat.

I gripped and twisted the blankets and began to cry. Maybe I should call my sister to come help me? I was too afraid to even reach for the phone. It was as if some force was sitting on me, surrounding me, suffocating my free will, my ability to physically move. I tried to talk back, but I couldn't.

You will never make it. You're a failure! The thoughts seemed to come in from out of nowhere, like gunshots in the dark. Were these my thoughts? They didn't sound like me. The voice was deep, guttural, threatening.

You are good for no one and it would be better if you would just leave this world.

I had no counterpoint, no defense. Whatever it was, this dark spirit began to take over and convince me that there was only one solution to this problem: I needed to take my own life.

How? I pictured myself heading down the stairs, going into the garage, shutting the doors, starting the car, putting down the windows and waiting patiently as the toxic fumes did their work. It wouldn't be pretty. It wouldn't be painless. But it would be relatively quick. And then it would be over.

I thought of my family. They loved me, of course, but they too would be better off without me. Wouldn't they? The force was so strong, so dark, so daunting, I felt like I had no option but to give in to it.

Be done! Quit!

I battled for control of my thoughts. The back and forth continued for what felt like an eternity. My sheets were soaked with tears and sweat, and I was shaking uncontrollably.

Go! Go now!

"Lord!" I called, suddenly finding my voice. "Please, come and deliver me! Deliver me from this darkness, from this fear!"

My voice escalated into a scream. I was falling fast, and I needed Him to rescue me. In my despair, I cried out and kept crying out for the only One who can save. And He did! The power of the Holy Spirit blanketed my bedroom and a smooth salve of peace came over me. My heart was still beating wildly, but my breathing began to slow and then normalize. I felt as light as if I'd just been released from heavy chains.

I knew it had to be some type of spiritual warfare. I had heard it preached about in church, but I'd never experienced it before. I looked at the clock. It was 5 a.m. The battle had been going on for hours, but now it was over. At that moment, I realized that my life did mean something. I was not a failure. I was suffering through a failure season. But that did not mean I was finished or that God couldn't still use me for something good.

The victory had been the Lord's. He had heard my cry, and in my darkest hour, He rescued me. Despite my mistakes, my pride, my shame, He still loved me and He had not given up on me. I let myself sink into that realization, and it comforted me.

Another long day stretched out in front of me.

I pulled the covers off and managed to get up and into the shower. As the hot water washed over me I started crying, a release of gratitude to God for delivering me from death. I had never encountered a battle like this with suicidal thoughts and a pit of despair that words cannot even begin to sufficiently describe. It's a dark place that is so paralyzing that only the power of an Almighty God can loosen its grip.

When God steps in, nothing is off limits, I thought. Just when you think you're walking the road all alone and unable to go on, He gives you exactly what you need.

I heard the phone ring. I quickly stepped out of the shower, grabbed my robe and managed to pick up the receiver before it went to voicemail on the fourth ring.

"Hello," I answered.

"Janet, this is Jim Rismiller."

It was my old basketball coach turned private school principal and accounting teacher.

I stood up a little straighter, suddenly feeling exposed and self-conscious.

"Well, hey, Jim, how are you?" I said, putting on my most normal, casual voice.

"I'm calling about that business of yours," he said. "I hear you could use some help."

SEVEN

FROM OUT OF THE PAST

And the LORD, He is the One who goes before you. He will be with you, He will not leave you nor forsake you; do not fear nor be dismayed. Deuteronomy 31:8

The mid-February air was even colder than usual when I steered into the pickup lane at Washington Dulles International airport. As usual, the narrow area was packed with cars, buses and people, and clouds of frosty condensation blurred the flight information display monitors. I silently willed the cab in front of me to move forward a bit so that I could get a better view of the passengers now pouring out of the terminal.

It was almost 9 a.m. Jim had caught the earliest direct flight out of Atlanta that morning, and he would be heading out of the arrivals building any moment now.

Lord, help this day to be productive, I prayed, keeping my eyes open, so I didn't somehow miss catching a glimpse of Jim in the crowd.

It had been five days since he'd called me in the immediate aftermath of my "dark night of the soul." Hearing his voice that morning had seemed surreal, and I had found myself momentarily speechless, completely amazed at the perfect timing of his call.

This was no coincidence, I thought. God was orchestrating a lighted path forward, sending me the exact person I needed at the exact right time. Jim was known as a whiz with finances, but more than that, he was tough and unafraid of a challenge. From my conversations through the years with Jeanette, Jim's wife, I knew that when faced with a mountain, Jim would march straight at it and not quit until he'd somehow found a way over.

"So, what do you say," he had challenged. "Do you want some help?"

"Sure, if you think you can," I replied. "But, you know, this is not an easy situation."

I was more than elated at his offer, but I didn't want to sugarcoat it and I certainly didn't want to waste his time.

"It will be okay," he said, softening his voice and peppering me with questions about the amount of debt I had, where we were with invoices and sales.

I could hear him scribbling some notes in the background. "Get me up there within the week and just let me get my hands around everything. If you'll work with me and listen to me, I'm confident we can get it all figured out."

The last time I had worked directly with Jim, I was a high school basketball player and he was my coach. I had gotten a taste of his management style—direct, decisive, sometimes loud—and I'd resented it.

Now, Jim was letting me know, in no uncertain terms, that he needed my full cooperation or there was no point in even continuing this conversation. Was I willing to accept those terms? I'd steered my own course for a long time, and I was used to making the final calls on all the major decisions that had to do with JANSON. But I'd been humbled by the events of the previous few weeks and now I knew my limitations.

"I'm all ears, Jim," I had promised.

A sudden knock on the back of my car jarred me out of my thoughts into the present. I looked in my rearview mirror and spotted Jim, crisply attired in a white shirt, dark slacks, a tie and a zip-up fleece. He gave a wave and walked over to the passenger side, opening the door, tossing his briefcase into the back and sliding into the seat next to me.

"Okay, let's go," he ordered.

"Agree," I said with a grin. "Let's get out of here."

I slipped the gear into drive, easing away from the curb and speeding away.

Jim was scheduled to catch a flight home at 6 p.m. that evening, so we had very little time to get a lot of work done. On his request, I had shipped him copies of key financial documents so he could get up to speed on JANSON's current state and also scheduled a meeting with the bank. I had set it for 10 a.m. that morning, which we would easily make if we didn't run into traffic.

"This invoice-buying business," he declared shortly after I'd accelerated out from behind a slow-moving car and into the passing lane on the Dulles Toll Road, "it stops right now."

I gulped and kept my eye on the road. I wasn't surprised that Jim, a by-the-book sort of person, would find my arrangement with the bank to be some kind of financial sacrilege, but those advances, however misguided, represented the only real cash flow I had right now.

"How will I pay JANSON's bills?" I questioned. "How will I pay you?"

"I'm going to help you," he explained. "And you clearly don't have the money to pay me at the moment, so don't worry about that right now. We got bigger problems to deal with."

He reached into the back and pulled out his briefcase, setting it on his lap and opening it up.

"How bad is it?" I asked. There was no point avoiding his verdict. "What are your thoughts?"

"Well, your accounts receivable are way out of balance compared to your accounts payable," he said. "And your spending is out of control. But I'm sure you knew that."

Yes, I knew. Oh boy, did I know! I gritted my teeth before clicking on the blinker and moving back into the driving lane in anticipation of an upcoming exit.

He continued. "This isn't something I haven't seen before. These are rookie mistakes, and you've gotten yourself into some pretty deep trouble. Here's the thing, though: I think your business has a future and a good one, but it's not going to be easy getting back on track. In fact, it's going to be painful for a while."

I glanced over at Jim. He was staring straight ahead, his jaw set like he was already envisioning himself standing at the foot of the steep mountain just ahead.

I sucked in some air and let it out slowly as I entered the exit lane for the next highway on our journey. *Thank you, Lord. Thank you for sending me this man.* Jim clearly had the emotional tenacity and the confidence that had been slowly drained out of me over the last few weeks. I was so beat down, so despairing. God knew I needed someone to pick me up and carry me for a while, and Jim was clearly the man for the job.

He reached under some files in his briefcase and pulled out a legal pad filled with copious notes. "I've got a bunch of questions for the banker," he said. "If you're okay with it, I'll lead the meeting."

"Absolutely," I said. A smile played on my face. I was thrilled to hand over the wheel.

We were early for the meeting with the bank manager, so an employee asked us to take a seat in the waiting area and offered to get us some coffee. I nodded, but Jim shook his head and sat down to continue going over his notes. Not wanting to disturb him, I took a seat across from him. When the employee returned with my coffee, I thanked her and wrapped my hands around the cup, not only to try and warm up but also to keep my hands from shaking.

As I watched Jim work, I wondered how I had so thoroughly misjudged him 15 years prior. The arrogance of youth was part of it, for sure, but my perspective had also been skewed by my general resentment of authoritative men. Now, after years as a business professional who had worked with and learned to deal with all types of people, I saw him very differently. There was no doubt, by any success metric, that Jim was an impressive person.

He had served in the Air Force for 25 years. He wasn't just military, though, he was "very" military, highly disciplined, quick to give and obey orders and sure of himself. He was also, in military parlance, a "mustang," an enlistee who displayed such leadership ability, such attention to detail and such dedication to his job that he'd been picked out of the crowd by the higher-ups and given an officer's commission. It was a rare feat. Without any pretension, though, Jim just kept going as he always did, excelling at every task, working his way up the officer chain and ultimately receiving his oak clusters and the rank of major. Throughout the course of his career, the only time Jim was called out by a superior was for working *too* hard—he was so driven in his daily tasks that he wasn't getting enough sleep.

Immediately after he retired, Jim took the position at my private high school. What a culture shock that must have been for him to go from giving orders to well-disciplined, obedient airmen to dealing with a bunch of rebellious, mouthy teenagers who were sure they knew more than he did, me being the absolute worst of the bunch.

He wasn't just my basketball coach, though. He coached other sports and taught accounting, and very soon—hardly a surprise—he started climbing the ladder, with promotions to athletic director then to director of finance and then headmaster.

I knew all of this because, even after I'd started at Orbital, I continued to go to church with Jim and Jeanette at the local church. While my relationship with Jim was more pleasant once I was out of school, it still remained largely distant. Jeanette and I, on the other hand, became close friends, despite the fact that we were very different. At that point, I was in my early 20s, and she was in her late 40s. I was still holding God at arm's length; she was totally committed to Him. I was brash, full of myself; she was steadfast, full of faith. And I was single, while she'd been happily married for decades.

She sought me out, I suspect, because of—and in spite of—my wild child reputation and attitude. I was known for having a great time, and I had such a mouth on me that I would sometimes slip words into my conversations that I was sure had never been part of her lexicon. I was a believer, but a nominal one, and it bothered her that I was sitting on the fence, unwilling to commit. Still, she lovingly counseled me, listened to me, laughed at my jokes, prayed with me and, in time, confided in me. Over time, I grew in my faith in large part because of Jeanette, and she grew to love me for the person I was and, just as importantly, the person I was becoming.

"You know, Jan," I recall her telling me in response to my constant striving for success as a businesswoman, "no matter where you go or what you go through, if you seek out God and walk with Him and seek His will, you will have a victorious life."

The relationship continued even after the Rismillers decided to move to Georgia to work at another private school, with Jeanette again teaching Spanish and Jim taking a position as operations director. I even traveled to their home in Georgia on occasion.

"Janet," I heard Jim say, pulling me out of my thoughts and pointing to the glassed-in office to our right. "It looks like the bank manager is wrapping up. Get ready."

I gathered my purse and briefcase, took another deep breath and put a smile on my face. It was time to play the part of the confident executive, no matter how unsettled I felt inside. "Got it," I told Jim. "You lead the way."

My conversation with the bank manager earlier that week had been void of any details, so I think he took it upon himself to assume that I was there to beg. As soon as I introduced him to Jim, "my new chief financial officer," and we all sat down, the banker started the meeting, clearly following his own agenda.

"Ms. Chihocky," he opened, looking directly at me and ignoring Jim. "I want to thank you for your recent payment getting your account up to date, but I have to say that we are concerned, very concerned, about your ability to pay going forward."

He was still in mid-thought when Jim took over. "Why?"

The bank manager stopped and stared at Jim for a moment, visibly irritated by the interruption, and then continued, still directing the conversation at me. "JANSON is clearly in trouble, Ms. Chihocky. You've got a big debt load with us. Your cash accounts have been drained. The last payment on the factoring arrangement was missed by several days, and there are more payments coming up."

He stared at me, and I felt uncomfortable. Although I wasn't behind in my payments, they could choose to call the home equity loan and the factoring advances at any time. That was his prerogative.

I worked to keep my anxiety to myself, smiling in his direction and looking to Jim to see how we would respond.

"Yes, the picture doesn't look great right now," Jim admitted. "But if you're wondering why I'm involved, let me tell you: I'm here to help her get back on her feet and help her turn this around. She's had a bad patch, but you don't attract the clients she has attracted and have the run rate she's had and somehow conclude that there is no future."

The man sat back in his chair. "Okay, Mr. Rismiller, what is your plan?"

"We need to formally close the factoring agreement. We won't be needing those services anymore," he stated.

"And the equity line of credit?"

"We'll be keeping that in place—until other arrangements can be made."

It was clear that Jim was in charge now. He had a plan, and he was already executing it. It was also clear that the bank manager didn't really care that he would eventually lose me as a customer.

"Fine," he said. "I'll get the paperwork."

I held a hand up as he rounded the desk and started toward the door. "Jim will be in charge of finances, so can you also get the papers you need for him to be a signatory on all of JANSON's accounts?" I smiled to ease the tension. "I'd really appreciate it."

The bank manager nodded and headed to a back office. Jim turned to me and stated bluntly, "We need a bank on our side—a bank that is patient, supportive and believes in you. This bank is not the bank we need."

He was right. Whether the bank manager believed that I could pull myself out of the hole or not really didn't matter. He'd made it clear that the bank didn't want our business anymore; his biggest concern was that we didn't do any bottom-line damage or put them out in any way before we moved on to another financier.

The bank manager came back into the office, and Jim signed the paperwork. "I'll be in touch," Jim said.

B ack at JANSON's office, my mother warmly greeted Jim. She had, of course, attended church with the Rismillers for years and she had always seen past Jim's terse style and recognized him for the decent, hard-working man he truly was.

"Who wants coffee?" She had brewed a large pot in anticipation of our return and didn't even wait for an answer before pouring two large, steaming mugs and handing one to each of us. "I've got sandwiches and snacks ready whenever you get hungry. Anything you need, just holler."

I smiled at her in gratitude. "If anyone calls, just take a message," I told her. "We're going to be heads-down unavailable for a while."

We worked at a small, round table in my office. Jim set down the preliminary file of key financial documents I'd already sent him, but now he wanted to see everything else. It was time, he explained, to "perform a complete dissection."

I dropped a big box of bills, invoices, credit card statements, financial reports and asset information in front of him, and he reached in and started pulling files out one after another, reading them quickly and taking notes.

Jim was deep in thought, so I took the time to move back to my desk to catch up on emails and other projects. Every once in a while, I would look up and watch him work. He was focused, efficient and organized. I could almost see his mind turning as he perused various figures and columns of numbers. *This is unbelievable*, I thought. Jim and I had never really been friends, yet here he was, sleeves rolled up, a real problem solver that God was using to re-energize me, to help me look forward, to help turn this around. God really did bring the right people, I thought, though never would I have thought it would be Jim. *Your plans, Lord, are definitely better than mine,* I thought.

After a couple of hours, Jim finally sat back, took off his glasses and rubbed his eyes. Then he put his glasses back on and picked up his notepad.

"Okay, let's talk," he said.

Sitting down next to him, I wrapped my hands around another cup of coffee, trying to soothe my nerves over whether or not there might be a surprise in this initial autopsy result.

"What do you think?" I asked. I wanted to wish this situation away, and parts of me had tried to deny it, but my mother hadn't raised me to run away from problems. This was my reality. Time to brace up to it.

It was bad, he admitted, but not hopeless. "The long goal is to get a consolidation loan under which we can structure all of the debt, but we can't do that overnight, and there's no guarantee you'll even be able to get one," he explained. "So in the meantime, we've got to get hold of some easy cash right away and then cut as many expenses as we possibly can without hurting sales and production."

He looked across all the files strewn across the table. "One thing I don't see is any information on your personal assets. You've probably still got a little equity in your house, I would imagine. Anything else?"

"Just my 401(k)," I said.

"Wait a minute—you've got money in a 401(k)? How much?"

"I don't know. $60,000, $70,000, I think." I had started dutifully putting money away for retirement when we first started JANSON, but since I wouldn't be needing it for another quarter century or so, I didn't keep a close eye on it.

"Well, that's even better," he insisted. "We'll tap that."

"But that's my retirement!" I protested.

Jim grinned. "Yeah, you're 32 years old. I don't think that's your biggest concern right now. I want you to get most of that money out, and we'll take the tax penalty. Leave a little in, but let's get the bulk of it."

He flipped a page on his legal pad and started a list of action items. Calling to get the retirement funds was at the top of the list.

"Now, once I get that, we can start to negotiate with some of your creditors."

Most companies, he explained, would agree to accept a lower amount, write off the loss and close out the account if they got a substantial payment upfront. In the long run, it was cheaper than chasing after the debt, and with JANSON teetering on the edge of bankruptcy, it aligned nicely with the practical principle that "getting something was better than getting nothing."

"We'll start with that money, but we still might have to pull some equity from your home, so you'll need to start looking into that in terms of how much is available and how long it will take to close on a loan," Jim ordered.

I suddenly felt anxious. This was definitely happening: I was gambling my savings and my security on a limping JANSON miraculously finding its feet and crossing the finish line victorious. It was more than a long shot. If we failed, my retirement would be gone, possibly my home. Was it worth the risk? What would happen to me if I failed again? My worries had grabbed the bit and were running away with me.

Jim seemed to read my thoughts. He tapped the table in front of me. "Right here, Janet, right now," he chided, drawing me back to the present. "Don't worry about tomorrow. Focus on right now."

He continued to write out a list. Next up, he wanted my

permission to call the landlord and try to negotiate out of the long-term lease on the office space I'd added the prior summer. We might have to pay a couple of months rent upfront, but it would save us in the long run.

He pulled out another file. "We need to cut as much as possible, wherever we can, to free up cash and get your overhead down," he declared. "Both professionally and personally."

Opening the file, he ran his finger down one of my credit card statements, which had already been marked up. "Who's Ann Taylor?" he demanded, mentioning the women's clothing store where I got the pricey designer suits that I couldn't quite resist.

"Oh, she's a friend of mine," I replied, smiling coyly.

He took a red pen to the entry on my credit card statement. "Find a way to get her out of your life," he ordered.

I knew there were plenty of other items on those statements that needed to be done away with: too many nights eating out, trips over long weekends, the occasional expensive gift for a friend or family member.

"I get it, Jim," I said, waving him off this particular project. "I'll put myself on a miserly budget."

"Good," he said, recognizing that since I would be living off of my personal savings account for who knows how long, I had plenty of motivation to cut my spending to the bone.

Next on the list, he explained that any client cash that came in would be frozen until the related project was finished. Getting money upfront for my invoices was one of many tactics that had set me up for failure, he explained, and it was probably the worst. Not only was JANSON paying a premium for that money in the form of interest to the bank, but the arrangement operated on the assumption that we would always receive the full amount of the invoices from the client.

I would spend that money on other expenses, but then if something went wrong with one of the ads or there was a dispute on the invoice or the client flat out refused to pay a portion, I had to make up the difference with new debt. It was a negative, destructive cycle.

Jim advised that, from now on, we would never again build our budget around the idea that JANSON could count on collecting all 100 percent of its projected revenue. "You can hope, but odds are you're only going to get 80 percent of it," he said. "And we have to plan for that, and that's how we're going to operate."

We hadn't even started tackling the debt that threatened to put the business under, but Jim was already showing his strong knack for planning and organization by putting structure and strong financial principles into place—in anticipation of future success. He was taking a step in faith.

By 3 p.m., we were wrapping up and finally took the time to eat a sandwich. "Here's the bottom line," Jim said between bites. "You start managing the pennies and the dollars will take care of themselves."

The platitude seemed counterintuitive given that we were talking about finding a way to pay down half a million dollars of debt. But that's how Jim rolled. He didn't have a lofty vernacular; he talked in simple, direct terms, but his financial and life philosophies were profound and always based on evidence, results and Biblical truth.

He was the strong, concerned, wise counsel I'd needed from the beginning, but better late than never.

For the next hour, Jim signed additional paperwork giving him authority to handle JANSON's financial affairs, and then we sent my mother off to make copies of various files and documents. He would work from his home in Georgia, and we would stay in close contact. He could always travel back if necessary.

As Jim gathered everything he needed to take with him, we didn't have everything figured out and our action list wasn't complete. Every day forward would give us new data to work with and new challenges to solve. But we had the loose structure of what we felt was a strong plan. The road would be long, but we were walking down it together, and we were optimistic. As we got back into the car late that day, we could both see a sliver of sunshine still peeking over the horizon.

By the time we pulled up to the curb outside the terminal at Dulles International airport late that afternoon, the sun had already gone down, and the frosty chill was again spawning clouds of condensation over the area as new crowds of people hurried across the sidewalk. I put the car in park and pulled my coat closer to my face.

"I'll be in touch," Jim said, grabbing his briefcase and placing a hand on the door handle.

Then he paused and turned back to face me. "Let me worry about all the financial stuff," he stated. "Anybody calls, you send them to me. You have any questions, you call me. Meantime, though, try to stay focused as much as possible on sales and the paying work. And take this one step, one task at a time. Don't let your worries pull you away from what we need to do right now. It will be okay."

"Got it," I chattered. Jim opened the door, stepped out and disappeared into the crowd.

I watched and waited until enough time had passed that I was sure he had made it into the terminal. At the beginning of all this, I had a full-time staff, a major accounting firm and a bank working on my behalf. Now I had just a few people on my side: Jim, my mother, and a couple of friends willing to volunteer from time to time. I couldn't help but think of the story of Gideon, who had headed out to fight the Midianites with a mighty army of 22,000 men, thinking that more was better. God thought differently. He ordered Gideon to use various means to determine who was truly committed, who was really ready to face the test. In the end, he went to battle with just 300 men, and it was enough.

Little is much when God is in it. I had an army of a few committed, supportive people who believed in our cause. Would it be enough? With God on my side, I was suddenly sure that it would be. And I would give Him the glory. Smiling at the thought, I put the car into gear and sped away.

CHAPTER 11

EIGHT

BUSINESS MATTERS

...when my heart is overwhelmed, lead me to the rock that is higher than I. Psalm 61:2

The morning after Jim flew back to Georgia, I sat down at my desk, pulled out the latest statement of my 401(k) retirement account and, running my finger down the page, quickly located the customer service number. We had a basic plan to save my company and I would waste no time putting it into motion. I dialed the number, eagerly tapping my pencil as I waited for the call to go through.

Okay, here goes, I thought, looking out the window and welcoming the unexpected warmth of the February sun as it rose higher in the sky. The phone began ringing, but it didn't even complete a second time before an automated teller answered and told me to listen closely to my options. Impatient, I bypassed the menu altogether by punching the "0" button, and after a short moment, a live voice came on the line.

"Good morning, can I get your account number?" I heard a woman ask in a professional but friendly voice.

Placing my finger under the information, I carefully recited each number. The representative then posed a series of personal and security questions, all designed to ensure that I was, in fact, who I said I was and authorized to discuss the account. Finally, satisfied with the information I provided, the representative replied, "Thank you, Ms. Chihocky. How can I help you today?"

"I want to withdraw $50,000 from my account."

It wasn't the full amount. The 401(k) was actually worth over $80,000, but Jim and I agreed that I should hang on to some of it. "There's no need to deplete it at this point," he had advised, and I too felt like we might need something to fall back on later.

I heard some typing in the background. "Okay," the representative said. "You do realize that since this is a tax-deferred retirement account, you will have to pay a 10 percent early withdrawal penalty and that this distributed amount will be added to your gross income and you will be taxed on that as well?"

"Yes, I understand." Jim and I had already calculated the amount. Poof! Just like that, thousands of my carefully set aside retirement dollars would disappear. The amount nabbed by government edict was harsh by design, intended to dissuade anyone from cracking open their nest egg before maturity.

"Would you like me to automatically calculate and withhold the penalty and associated state and federal tax for you?" she continued.

"Yes, please do that," I told her.

The representative asked me to verify my Social Security number and then explained that she would be mailing some papers for me to sign. As soon as I returned them, the company would mail me a check.

"Please send everything by priority mail or FedEx," I insisted. "I'd like to get this completed as quickly as possible."

She said she would. I thanked her and hung up.

Within days, the check arrived, and I hustled over to the bank to deposit it in my personal account. Once that was completed, I wrote out another personal check to JANSON and handed it to the teller, asking her to deposit it into the main business account.

That evening, I informed Jim that we were good to go. He was now JANSON's official Chief Financial Officer, though I wasn't paying him a dime, and from this point on I could send every phone call and every document that involved finances to him. Finally, I could let go of all the things that had been dragging me down and holding me under. Now, I was free to focus on the business development, the creative production, the program management and the client relationships—all the business functions I loved doing and did well.

The primary goal initially was to stop the bleed enough to buy time and give us room to breathe. In the weeks before Jim came on board, I was no longer able to pay JANSON's most basic operational bills in full, including electricity and rent. We were running up new arrearages that offered no grace period, and we were probably weeks, if not days, from getting threats of turn-off and an eviction notice.

Now, though, with some cash in hand, Jim would be able to "start cleaning up aisle 9," as I liked to say, and one day, hopefully, start working on aisles 1 through 8.

Jim had a full-time teaching and administrative job at another private school in Georgia, but as soon as his day job was done, he would head home and go to work for JANSON. When the persistent debt collectors called into our office, we immediately re-routed them to Jim, who, in his usual pithy, direct style, helped them to understand that he was the CFO and would be back in touch with *them* when *he* had something to report.

Jim had designed a general plan forward for the cash I

received from my 401(k), and like the disciplined Air Force officer he had once been, he now carried it out one logical, unwavering, matter-of-fact step at a time. First up, Jim sat down and wrote all the checks required to catch us up on outstanding fixed monthly expenses, including electricity, rent, insurance and other critical bills. He paid the invoices, both due and overdue, and he took care of the payroll, which now comprised just a single employee, my mother, who worked as both administrative assistant and head cheerleader.

Access to cold, hard cash was power in more ways than one, and Jim leveraged that power deftly and strategically. One key move he made was to get us out from under the cost of the extra office space I'd taken on the previous year. In a negotiation with the landlord, Jim offered to pay three months rent upfront for those additional offices if he would, in exchange, release us from the multi-year lease. The landlord was happy to take the deal since he was free to immediately try to lease the offices to another firm. We were out another chunk of my dwindling 401(k) cash, but in the long-term, ostensibly, we would save money—and a lot of it.

Next, Jim began tackling the debt. We were up to our necks in it. He was able to negotiate JANSON out of a few older, smaller obligations, but his biggest concern was devising a plan for dealing with the larger debt liabilities. We had started climbing the mountain, but now, in my mind, we were standing at the bottom and looking up at a near-vertical rock face. Without the right strategy, tools and attitude, it might stop us dead in our tracks.

Of course, I was the one who had brought us to this point. I had run up the debt and I had mismanaged the finances. But Jim owned it with me. Even though he hadn't created the problem, he was just as committed to solving it as I was, and that support gave me confidence. For so long, I had to shoulder the responsibility for all of the business functions, and that reality had made me a reactive executive, much too focused on putting out fires and crossing items off of daily to-do lists rather than creating and carrying out a larger business vision.

In Jim, I instantly had the business partner I had long felt I needed. He had the experience, the competence and the drive to handle not just the accounting and financial management concerns but also the larger administrative and operational tasks. Already, he was thinking strategically, well beyond our current conundrum, and putting in place stronger, more disciplined processes and structure for cash flow management and fiscal planning.

That support freed me up to focus on the billable work, identify new business and better manage all of the client relationships. But it was more than that. For the first time since I'd started the business, I was able to start taking a big-picture view of JANSON. I was able to think strategically, rather than just tactically: How could I drive new demand for the business? What did I need to do to better develop proposal templates and strategies to sustain my current clients and win new ones?

Finding a way out from under the debt was still threatening to topple the company, but even as we chipped away at the weight of it, we were tending to the foundational principles of what makes up a healthy, sustainable business. If we succeeded in finding a way forward, JANSON could potentially come out stronger than it had ever been—and extremely well positioned for future growth and success.

As the days went by, the communication and respect between Jim and me only improved. Here I was, flailing in this deep pit, and Jim was the one who had willingly jumped in to help me work my way out of it. We both worked with a sense of urgency and initiative, each in our own lane, each doing what we did best. Jim respected that I had been willing and able to step out and start a business at a relatively young age in a highly complex, highly technical market, and I was in awe of his accounting craft and his willingness to tackle any hard mountain he believed was worth crossing.

One afternoon, as we talked on the phone and looked over JANSON's liability statement, I asked him, "So what *are* we going to do about these big bills that we need to start paying down?" I asked. I tried to sound confident but inwardly, as I stared at the massive, multi-digit numbers in front of me, I worried that I might start hyperventilating.

"Don't worry," Jim replied calmly, picking up on my anxiety through the phone line. "I'm going to negotiate both sides of the aisle. We'll get it worked out."

These little snippets of encouragement were often just the therapy I needed to calm down, refocus and get back to the work at hand. When I found myself ruminating on the "what if's"—What if we can't consolidate our debts? What if the bank calls the biggest loan? What if we don't make it?—I would pray for a moment and then immediately remember the encouragement I'd gotten from so many people along the way, people who seemed to show up with the right words at just the right moment. Like the smart advice my friend Karen had given me early on: "When times are good, your business is demonstrating that it is committed to you. However, when times are difficult, that is when you show that you are committed to your business."

The fact was, regardless of the overwhelming debt, regardless of the mistakes I'd made, regardless of the betrayal I'd experienced and regardless of how many unpaid hours I had to work to get out of this dilemma, the business of JANSON mattered to me. It mattered a lot!

As Jim and I faced this uphill battle, I vowed that I would

continue to take every painful step necessary and keep moving forward. It was hard going at times, but I was not going to let myself down, I was not going to let my clients down and I especially was not going to let God down.

And so it continued throughout the month. Jim spent his afternoons negotiating and settling debts and his evenings pouring over my books to find new ways to cut. The man clearly had a gift for finances, not the least of which was how to stretch a dollar!

"This month's electric bill was $6 higher than last month's," he bluntly informed me one day. "Are you leaving any lights on at night?"

Six dollars? Really? Given the enormity of what we were dealing with, it seemed like a petty point, but Jim really did care about every dollar, every little detail. It added up, and in time, I found that I cared as well.

Increasingly inspired and confident, I spent most of my days managing every project, working with every client, leveraging my network for new clients and maximizing every marketing capability I possessed.

Now that Jim was on board, I could turn my full attention to really knowing the complex markets in which my clients competed, which were changing rapidly due to the expanding Global War on Terror, the resulting push for a consolidated Homeland Security Department and the recession—all of which were combining to force a wave of new mergers and acquisitions throughout the aerospace and defense industries.

My business was in trouble, but if we did manage to survive, my clients needed me to understand this new market, to know what the next big thing was going to be and how they would be positioned within it. I needed to be able to find their unique differentiators, craft the right messaging to capture that uniqueness and then provide guidance and strategic structure to my creative team so we could show and tell that story effectively in ads, brochures and web pages. All of that required a lot of planning and a lot of research on my part. So in between ongoing work and my phone calls with Jim, I poured over business newspapers and trade publications, I sat in on technical seminars and I worked the crowds at industry events.

All the while, I stayed true to my clients and their needs. I didn't sell just to sell. If I did not believe that something would benefit a client and their mission, I did not suggest it. I valued relationships, and JANSON was a relationship business. In the end, I believe that is why every client continued to stick with us. They knew that I valued them, that I cared about their business, and they trusted that, even under the most trying of circumstances, I would be loyal and continue to tend to their needs.

So with Jim in his sweet spot and me in mine, we made a formidable team. He called me daily to let me know exactly what he was planning to do or had done. When he had a new idea about an area to cut or a new thought on how to move forward, he always bounced it off of me, patiently explaining the whys and wherefores of what he was thinking. He always took a strong hand to whatever task was before him, but I never felt like he was taking over. He could be curt, but he was never condescending. He was steadfast, and when my optimism waned or I began to have doubts, Jim would pick me back up.

"Focus on what you need to do, right here, right now," he would order, "not on the 'what ifs.' You can't do anything about those."

Away from the office in my personal life, I resolved to live just as tightfistedly. With no paycheck coming in for the foreseeable future, I had to stretch my savings account for as many months as possible. I was determined to do exactly that—but it would mean living a very different lifestyle from that to which I'd grown quite accustomed.

To make it happen, I worked to incorporate into my own personal budget Jim's favorite financial philosophy: *Manage the pennies. The dollars will take care of themselves.* It seemed counterintuitive. I had long pulled in a healthy salary and a comfortable lifestyle that included shopping, vacations, dinner with friends, the occasional trip to a spa. Cutting those things out would be relatively easy, but could putting my spending habits under a microscope and scrimping in even the most mundane areas of my life really make that much of a difference? I would soon find out.

Inside my home, I opened a filing cabinet, grabbed a chunk of personal finance folders and placed them on the dining room table. Sitting down, I flipped through them briefly and then sighed. There was no point trying to chisel my way through this mess. It required an axe, and I resolved to chop from my daily life and my monthly budget just about anything that wasn't included on the lowest rung of Maslow's hierarchy of human needs: air, water, sleep, food, shelter and transportation. The last one wasn't actually on Maslow's list, but it was critical for my survival since I needed a way to get around the far-flung sprawl that was northern Virginia.

I pulled out a legal pad and drew up a short list of absolutes: the mortgage, electricity, phone, water, car payment and car insurance. Putting my pen down, I set aside those files and began exploring what was left. "Clothing," read one file that was loaded up with receipts from local retail outlets. Buying anything new was definitely out, but I also resolved to rely on wash-and-wear outfits for regular office days that didn't involve client meetings. That would save a hefty amount on my dry-cleaning costs. I picked up another file: "Gas." I could significantly cut that expense by driving only when absolutely necessary or carpooling when possible. I put the file at the bottom of the pile and glanced at the next one: "Tithing." What did 10 percent of nothing equal? I certainly couldn't give my church as much as I once had, but I vowed to try to give what I could each Sunday. It was the right thing to do.

Reaching the bottom of the pile, I saw the final title: "Obdura Family." I looked up at my surroundings and felt a pang of guilt. I had a stove, a refrigerator, nice furniture, pretty paintings on the wall, all luxuries by Kenyan standards. Even if JANSON didn't make it, I would be fine. I could get another job, even sell my house and move in with my mother. But the Obduras? Without my monthly subsidy, Daisy and her children would be without the most rudimentary of human needs: food and shelter. The most recent letter I'd received had relayed devastating news: Daisy had contracted AIDS. The prognosis was not good, and I shuddered to think of what would happen to the children.

"No way!" I said out loud. Their needs were just as important as mine, and I would not abandon them. They had been such a blessing to me. I recalled Daisy singing in the choir, a young widow and mother, full of strength and faith in the face of such hardship, still eager to sing loudly and passionately about Jesus and His mercy. I felt tears begin to well up in my eyes, and I reached for a tissue.

"Thank you, Jesus, for bringing this family into my life," I told Him. "I claim them in Your Name. I know that You will continue to provide what I need to help them."

I pulled the legal pad out from under the files and wrote down the Obdura donation on my list of must-pays.

From that point on, I lived like any other kind of dieter. I did away with bad habits and created new ones, like packing my own lunch, keeping my credit card at home and watching movies on television rather than going out. I did without whenever possible, but I struggled to adjust to the sudden deprivation. I took those early days and weeks moment by moment. It kept me from getting too overwhelmed.

Three weeks into my new system, a friend asked me to go for dinner and a movie, Dutch treat, of course. Eager for a break from the very long, frustrating days at JANSON and in need of support, socialization and a good laugh, I counter-offered: "I can't make the movie, but how about we meet for an early dinner?" Instead of an entrée, I opted for a bowl of soup, a small indulgence that paid dividends to my morale.

Mom, of course, did all she could to ease my burden. She occasionally dropped a bag of groceries at my house and frequently invited me to dinner. "Come on over!" she'd insist. Like Jim, she was intimately familiar with how to stretch a dollar. At least I was getting one decent, hot meal on occasion—and a respite from my nutritional mainstay of peanut butter and jelly sandwiches.

By late March, we were ready to start applying for a consolidation loan. "We need a bank," Jim stated. It had become his mantra, something he repeated whenever we got into a conversation about how things were going and where we were headed.

I came up with a list of six local banks that frequently advertised their eagerness to lend money, even to those whose financial status wasn't optimal. My first choice seemed the most promising, a small institution known simply as "The Small Business Bank." If any bank would be willing to lend a hand, it had to be this one, right? A consolidation loan was our ticket out of our debt mess, so I could hardly contain my excitement as I dialed a nearby branch, booked a meeting with a business banker and pulled together all of the required paperwork. As I breezed into the lobby a few days later, wearing a smart, spring-style business suit and a sunny smile, I was dressed for success and a "Yes! We'd love to help you, Ms. Chihocky."

When the banker walked out to greet me, he shook my hand and returned my smile. He seemed friendly enough, offering me a cup of coffee and pulling out the chair a little further from the conference table so I could more easily maneuver the large file case I was carrying.

"Okay, great. Let me take a look at your financials," he said. I pulled out a folder containing all of my summary documents: balance sheet, current bank statements, income and profit and loss statements and a list of clients and ongoing projects. He reached across and took them. He situated his glasses and smiled again briefly, before taking on a let's-get-down-to-business look and leaning forward to browse my numbers. I looked out the window and tried to relax. So far, so good, I thought. Within minutes, though, I couldn't help but recognize that all manner of frowns, sighs and paper shuffling were pointing to a resounding "No!"

"I'm sorry, Ms. Chihocky. Your numbers just don't meet our criteria, so I'm afraid I can't help you," he said, standing up to let me know the meeting was now over. He reached out to shake my hand. "I wish you the best of luck, though."

When I called Jim and told him the news, he quietly listened as I recounted the morning's events and my deep sense of disappointment. "Why do these banks advertise that they are here to help the small guys when in reality if you don't check all of their boxes, you get nothing? What happened to the days when banks took the time to get to know you and your business and take a little risk on somebody who's trying?" I fumed. "They're so eager to throw money at you when you don't need it, but when you do need it, they slam the door in your face!"

Jim quickly lost patience with my rant. "Let it go, Janet," he clucked at me. "We knew this wouldn't be easy. We need a bank—but we don't need a bank that doesn't believe in the company or doesn't believe in you. Just get ready for the next time."

I knew he was right, and I tried to stay focused on the moment. As I recalled from the Gospel of Matthew, each day provided me with enough troubles—I didn't need to reach ahead for new ones. I spent the rest of the week researching and doing business development for JANSON, working with the team of consultants to make sure the products we were turning out remained in line with our quality standards and discussing next steps with Jim.

By the following week, I was geared up to apply for another consolidation loan with the next bank on my list. It pretty much went the same way as my first meeting, though, this time with a different face and in a different place, and the scenario repeated itself once again two weeks later. I tried to remain upbeat, but I felt as tired as if I'd run a marathon—only I hadn't gotten anywhere.

Jim called a few days later, ready to take another, parallel step in our plan. "It's time—we're going to need to tap the equity in your home," he stated. "I don't need it yet, but it's probably going to take a while to get it done, so get started."

We had stopped the bleed, but we were still drowning in debt. "Right," I said. This was a task that had already been signed off on, had already been put into action. Now I just needed to pull the trigger. "I'm on it."

I contacted the bank that held my mortgage, and this banker was actually eager to work with me. Historically, home equity loans were a low risk for lenders. They expected I would either pay it back over time or, if I ever sold my house, in one fell swoop.

What's more, in the spring of 2002, despite the ongoing recession, interest rates were low and housing values were rising rapidly across the country. Banks, including the bank that held my loan, were keen to be a part of this boom. In my case, a loan wasn't contingent on my current and potential earning capability but rather on that of my townhouse. In the high-demand and low-supply housing market of Northern Virginia, home prices for the last twenty years followed a single direction—up. My house was no exception. An appraisal ordered by the loan officer found that it was now worth significantly more than I owed on it.

The bank, the loan officer declared, was more than happy to lend me half of that amount and hold the remaining equity as collateral. Whether I paid my loan as expected or whether I defaulted, the lender, by their calculation, couldn't lose.

I was elated. Every business owner needs to be prepared for this time when they might have to put it all on the line, and that time had come. With all I'd already done, there was no stopping now. Bringing my house to the table to pull equity from it was just the next step. The following Saturday morning, I hopped into my car and headed to the bank to sign the paperwork. I couldn't wait to close the deal. It was a gorgeous day, not too hot and not too cold, and I had already planned to take a break from the pressures of work by spending the day sightseeing with my good friend Jeanne, who never failed to make me laugh and see the brighter side of life.

When the banker placed a stack of 20-plus pages in front of me, handed me a pen and began to explain what and where I needed to sign and initial, however, I hesitated.

This is it, I thought, suddenly feeling the full weight of this decision. I was about to take my home out of play and put it into peril. If JANSON didn't make it, my safe place, my comfort zone, my most valuable worldly asset, would likely be gone with it. *Is this really what God wanted me to do?*

Sensing that maybe I didn't quite understand his instructions, the loan officer tried to nudge me along, pointing to the bottom of the page where a short line was highlighted with yellow marker and a large "X."

"We just need your initials right here on this first page, Ms. Chihocky," he directed, tapping the page.

I looked at him and then set my pen down on the desk. "I'm sorry," I said. "Can you give me a minute?"

A flash of confusion and irritation crossed his face before he relented. "Of course. Take your time. I'll just go get a cup a coffee."

When the door shut behind him, I silently bowed my head and prayed. *Lord, I believe, in faith, that this is Your will for me, so unless You direct me otherwise, I am signing this paperwork and trusting You for the outcome.*

I lifted my head, sat back and felt a feeling of total peace wash over me. "Thank you, God," I whispered, looking up. I grabbed the pen and began initialing each page, not stopping even when the banker walked back into the office, sat down and thumped his coffee cup on the desk. Reaching the bottom of the stack, I signed and dated the final page. I looked up at the banker and smiled. His face visibly relaxed and he finished what was likely a rehearsed script. The funds, he explained, would be deposited and available for use by the following day. He handed me my copies of the paperwork and told me that if I needed anything else, I could call him any time. I reached across the desk and stuck my hand out. "Thank you," I said, meaning it, before picking up my purse and walking out. I never looked back.

I felt good now. I had checked another box on the to-do list, even though I still had what would feel like another 100 to go.

Within a few weeks, I had tried and failed three more times with my highest priority task. I contacted the final three banks on my list to apply for a consolidation loan for JANSON, but one by one, bankers welcomed me into the office, asked for my financial records, gave me hope and then politely but firmly rejected my request.

The implication was clear. No bank wanted to work with me. JANSON, to their mind, was the ultimate risk, pure poison, a company deep in debt and still limping along at half-speed.

"Hang in there," the loan officer at the last bank told me as he handed my various financial statements back to me. "I believe you can turn this thing around, but unfortunately, we cannot help you at this time."

In the car afterward, I bowed my head and gave it all over to God. "Give me patience, Lord," I said. "Six doors have slammed in my face, but isn't seven your favorite number?"

Jim remained undeterred. With the new home equity money in hand, he continued to chip away at his action list, negotiating us out of as many small debts as possible, finding additional ways to trim spending and building even more discipline and healthy habits into the company's financial operations. We *were* making headway. But somehow, someway, we had to get the debts consolidated. JANSON couldn't survive otherwise.

We needed a bank, to be sure, but what we really needed was a banking relationship.

— NINE —

FUEL FOR THE JOURNEY

For He has given you the former rain faithfully, and He will cause the rain to come down for you....You shall eat in plenty, and be satisfied, and praise the name of the Lord your God, who has dealt wondrously with you.... Joel 2:23, 26

I stood in the doorway as, one by one, 30 women wandered into a large classroom tucked away in the basement of the local Baptist church. "Hey, good morning!" I greeted each of them, smiling broadly and giving hugs and following up with a variety of upbeat messages. "It is so good to see you....It's a beautiful day, isn't it?.... You look great in that outfit!"

For some time now, I'd been leading a Sunday School class, and despite my preoccupation with JANSON's financial troubles and being often overwhelmed by 60- and sometimes 70-hour workweeks, I was still showing up each Sunday. This year, I was teaching a devotional study called "Falling in Love with Jesus," which had been co-authored by the Christian singer and songwriter Kathy Troccoli and well-known author and Bible teacher Dee Brestin.

I wasn't here out of a sense of obligation to the women who were now sitting at long tables, flipping through their workbooks and Bibles and patiently waiting for me to start the session. The truth was, they didn't need me nearly as much as I needed them. The class was something I could pour into each week for strength and renewal. No matter how bad things had been, coming here, connecting with these women, talking about Jesus, always took me to a different place—a place of hope, a place of revival. Teaching Sunday School gave me fuel for the journey. It gave me perspective. Most importantly, it brought me closer to God.

"Okay, who wants to start us off with a word of prayer?" I asked. One woman in the back row raised her hand. "Wonderful, thank you," I responded, bowing my head as she asked God to be with us during this time, to provide a greater understanding of who He is and to help us as we sought to have a stronger relationship with Him.

It had been a few years since my pastor had asked me to consider leading a Bible study for working women, most of whom were my age and older. At the time, I'd thought it premature. Me? Teach? About the Bible? By then, I had made a serious, committed transition from nominal Christian to true believer, but I still felt a little too young, a little too immature in my faith. Many of my "students" would be in their 40s and 50s, most boasting a well-tested faith and decades of career experience—not to mention husbands, children and, in some cases, grandchildren. Who was I to lead them?

Sensing my hesitation, the pastor had encouraged me. "Pray about it, Janet. The thing is: The teacher is almost always the one who ends up growing the most."

He'd been right. To prepare for my class each week, I spent a lot of time during my evenings digging deeper into the Word, praying for guidance and being much more purposeful. And I soon found that teaching and motivating was a great fit for me.

As was evident even in my earliest years in high school, I had a gift for getting the attention of an audience, whether it included 30 or 300 participants. My high school public speaking coach had brought that out in me. He taught me how to own the subject and how to let my passion shine through. But teaching was more than just getting up and holding forth on a topic and persuading people to understand the subject matter or your unique point of view.

Teaching, especially in the Sunday School format, was much more collaborative, more impactful. I could be inspiring, motivating and humorous in how I presented the topic at hand, but I could also pose questions, encourage a discussion, bring people out of their shells, put my own emotions into the topic. Most importantly, I got to learn—and learn a lot.

I loved it! And those ladies were always a blessing to me— though never more than during this spring as I struggled to keep JANSON afloat and find a financial way forward. Through the previous years, teaching Sunday School had helped me to grow tremendously in my understanding of God's character and in my faith in His promises. But as I transitioned from relatively calm waters into the rough rapids of uncertainty and peril, I needed to lean more fully into that character, and I needed to learn not only to be hopeful about those promises but to fully trust in them—even though a return to more tranquil waters was nowhere in sight.

I never hid my struggles from my Sunday School students, and they were never anything but supportive and encouraging. They asked about my week and my progress. They brought in cards of support—and often I'd get cards in the mail during the week reminding me that I was in their thoughts and prayers.

"Okay, let's turn to page 98 in your workbooks," I directed. Here, the focus was on Mary, who is sitting at the feet of Jesus, while her sister, Martha, is in the kitchen slaving away over lunch.

"How irresponsible!" I contend. "You know that's what Martha is thinking. You know she's slamming down pots and pans, dropping really noisy hints, so Mary gets how badly she's slacking off. You know, we'd probably be thinking it too. Here I am, in here, doing all this work, making sure that Jesus is comfortable, has something to eat, and she's in there, fawning over Him, trying to get to know Him better, trying to understand Him. What good is that doing? Now, who can relate? How many of us are so busy with our 'to do' lists, with taking care of everyone else, with being busy, busy, busy all the time, that we don't take time to spend any time with Jesus? How are we supposed to get to know Him? And how can we fully love Him if we don't know Him?"

I looked around and saw a lot of nodding heads. "That's definitely me," I admitted. "It's hard for me to sit quietly with God. Sometimes I actually have to write it on my 'to do' list in order to get it done, and the whole time, I'm thinking off to the side: 'This is all great, but in the meantime, I need to do this, and then I need to do that.' But it shouldn't be that way. We should want to spend time with Him. That's what He wants. He wants us to *want* to be with Him—just like we want Him to be with us."

Around the room, the women nodded, with a few raising their hands to share how their own daily tasks and need for feeling useful and active made their relationship with God more shallow, more distant.

Relationships had always been important to me. I cherished the relationships I had with my mother, siblings, extended family and friends. I always enjoyed helping others: when someone is in need, you act, you give, you do what's requested, what's necessary. As the class got deeper into the study, I had realized that relationships, even with God, had to be both give and take. But they weren't just about action. They were also strengthened and deepened by mere presence, by the effort to connect with and understand each other.

I also realized that no relationship was more important than my relationship with Christ. He is the vine and we are the branches, as Jesus Himself had so colorfully pointed out in the 15th chapter of John. Without the vine, the branch is dead. I couldn't bear fruit on my own. I couldn't even begin to blossom without Him. I needed that connection, and I needed it to be strong, unimpeded and endless.

And so that spring as I struggled to keep JANSON going, as I dealt with debt and rejection and uncertainty, I doubled down on my relationship with Christ. I nurtured it and challenged it through the preparation and teaching of this Sunday School class. I carved out more time for reading His Word, for prayer. I spent my evenings repeatedly listening to Sandi Patty songs that reminded me that *He* is the One who sets me free from all of my "yesterdays." Throughout the day, I recognized His faithfulness in the smallest of gestures and coincidences. And as I poured out my fears and concerns to Him, just as I would a close friend or loved one, I could noticeably feel Him taking the weight of my business off of my shoulders and carrying it for me.

As I finished the class that day and as everyone was gathering their pens and workbooks and Bibles and hurrying off to the regular church service, one woman hung back. She then walked over to me, hugged me and palmed $20 into my hand. "This isn't much," she told me, "just a little something to let you know that I'm thinking of you."

My old prideful but insecure instincts would have told me to refuse her, to give it back, but I realized that however small a gesture, it was a true blessing because she gave it from her heart. More importantly, it was a timely blessing. I needed some personal encouragement, that little extra boost.

"Thank you so much," I whispered. I was learning how to receive and how to appreciate the little things. And I was realizing that God never fails. He always gives you exactly what you need the moment you need it.

A fter the sixth bank rejected me, I should have been in despair. Not a single banker had been willing to take me beyond the initial application phase, and now my shortlist of possibilities had been reduced to zero. Every carefully selected entry had a line slashed through it. Were we nearing the end? Was this it?

Not as far as I was concerned. I had long felt led by God to keep going, not to close the door, but, to be honest, patience had never been my strong suit. And for a little while, it got worse. That's because for so long, it seemed that nothing was really happening. We were running hard but getting nowhere. My emotions often got out in front of my faith. I was still beating myself up for the mistakes I'd made in the past.

One night, as I prayed, I suddenly had this thought run through my brain, as clearly as if God Himself were sitting in front of me and counseling me: *Yes, I have promised to deliver you, but my promises are not going to be fulfilled according to your timetable.* The conclusion was obvious: God had never told me how or when deliverance would come, just that it would come—in His time.

With that, I worked to put one foot in front of the other, to stay fully focused on the right here, right now. Jim was still taking care of the finances, so I needed to continue to focus on my part: working with the clients, doing the work that needed to be done right now and identifying and developing new business opportunities.

In the meantime, I needed to simply wait on the Lord, but wait *patiently*. It took a while, but I was learning how to do just that.

Doors were slamming shut everywhere I turned, and every day seemed to bring some type of new trial and test. My impatient, controlling self still wanted to jump in. I wanted to learn my lessons as quickly as possible and move on. But I was beginning to gain a sense of peace too that God had me where I was for a reason; He was helping me work through and begin to heal deep-rooted issues, and this season of adversity would jumpstart that process faster than any amount of success ever could.

I couldn't see an easy solution in sight. But I was beginning to accept that God would come through, that He would do it in His own time—and that I would be better off because of the wait, not in spite of it.

A few weeks later, I was heading back to the office on Route 234 when I noticed a First Union Bank branch off to my left. I'd probably passed it a hundred times but had never really taken note of it. Despite being one of the biggest banks in the country, it somehow hadn't made my list of banks. How had I overlooked it?

When I got back to the office, I searched for the number for the specific branch I'd passed by and called. It couldn't hurt to ask, I thought, twirling around in my chair to look out the window. The overcast sky didn't tell the whole story: It was hot today, one of the hottest days so far this year.

A female teller answered on the third ring. I barely let her finish her scripted greeting when I asked, "Who is your business banker?"

"Oh, that would be Beth," she said, clearly eager to be helpful. "Would you like me to put you through to her?"

"Yes," I replied. "Thank you so much."

I again began nervously tapping my pen in anticipation. Six up, six down. I refused to give up. Come on, No. 7!

"Good afternoon, this is Beth Jenkins," she answered in a voice that was warm and friendly. "How can I help you?"

"Hi, Beth, this is Janet Chihocky," I announced, using my most confident, executive-sounding tone. "I am the CEO of JANSON Communications, a small marketing communications company here in Prince William County. If possible, I'd like to set up a time to meet with you sometime in the next week to discuss a business loan."

There was a brief silence, and through the receiver, I could hear the sound of paper being shuffled. I held my breath as I waited for her to respond.

"Of course, I'd be happy to meet with you," she said. "How about early next week, say, Tuesday, 10 a.m.?"

"Perfect," I replied. "I'll be there."

"Actually," she countered. "Why don't I come to you? I'd love to see your offices, get a sense of the kind of work you do."

Now that was a new one on me. The business bankers I'd met with before didn't really care what JANSON actually did; they only wanted to see how it looked on paper, to determine how, and if, the numbers added up. Of course, those calculations didn't even begin to tell the whole story. Perhaps Beth actually understood that and could see that the company had a future.

"Absolutely, I would love to have you come visit JANSON," I gushed, before quickly catching myself and forcing a more professional pitch.

I provided her with the company's street address and phone number. Then I offered to send her JANSON's financial statements. "It will give you a chance to get up to speed on where we're at before our meeting," I suggested.

My proactive offer wasn't just for her benefit. If First Union had some kind of predetermined loan criteria that JANSON didn't meet, if our numbers were too square to fit into inflexible round holes, I wanted to know sooner rather than later. There was no point in wasting anybody's time, least of all mine.

"That's a wonderful idea," she agreed. "Yes, please send them along."

After getting her mailing address and exchanging a few more pleasantries, I hung up and immediately set about pulling together the relevant paperwork, packaging it up and running it out to a nearby FedEx office. As I slipped the package into the slot and let it go, I said a prayer. *We just need one bank, Lord Jesus, one banker who cares. Let this one be the one.*

If anyone could tell the JANSON story, it was me. I knew the markets, the client targets we needed to pursue, the hit we took in the aftermath of the 9/11 terror attacks, my vision for the future. Why hadn't I been able to get anyone to take an interest, to take a chance on JANSON?

A day before my scheduled appointment with First Union, John, a client, called me to talk about a project I was working on for his firm, a major aerospace company. He was a brilliant manager and strategist, and it was my job to effectively support his company as it navigated a complex, ever-changing marketplace. Still, he always managed to turn the tables on me, asking me about JANSON and offering encouragement and sage advice. He had become an amazing supporter to me during this difficult time. He was someone who was willing to hear about the pain of my situation but without getting nervous about its potential impact on *his* company. As usual, his phone call that morning was right on time. I really needed a good pep talk.

"How are things going with JANSON?" he asked after we'd wrapped up our discussion of his project. "What's going on?

So I told him about my upcoming meeting with the seventh bank. For all of my speaking and teaching abilities, I know I hadn't done a good job of selling JANSON in my other bank meetings. I needed to do better.

"Janet," he advised gently, "no matter how desperate you are for the money, don't be desperate in your presentation. Be confident, be focused, but don't ever let her see you sweat."

I took his advice to heart, and in the moments before Beth arrived, I was ready. I had a smile on my face, and I was completely relaxed. The past was behind me, and this morning was all that mattered: I was staring at a chance for a "Yes!" *Give me the right words, Lord,* I prayed. *Let her see JANSON for its capabilities, for its potential, not just the problems it is currently having.*

Beth arrived at exactly 10 a.m. I heard her clear, engaging voice when she announced herself after walking in and up to the reception desk. "Good morning. I'm Beth Jenkins, and I'm here to see Janet Chihocky."

"Well, hello," my mother replied. "I'm Janet's mom."

"Hello, Janet's mom. It is very nice to meet you. You must be so proud of your daughter."

The two were chatting like old friends by the time I was able to put away a few papers, get out from behind my big desk and walk the short distance to the reception area. Beth turned to me, and I was immediately taken by her big, warm smile, which she flashed at me while stepping over to shake my hand. "Janet! So nice to finally meet you. What a wonderful office you have. My, you look so young, and you've started your own business!"

I felt immediately comfortable with her. "It's nice to meet you as well," I said.

As we started towards my office, Mom suddenly asked, "Beth, would you like a cup of coffee or tea before you get started?"

"That would be wonderful," she said. "Coffee, please." Mom caught my eye, and after I nodded, she turned and disappeared.

I led Beth into my office, but instead of following me directly to the small round table near my desk, she lingered along a wall. On that wall, I had framed and hung numerous examples of the creative work that JANSON had crafted for major aerospace companies, as well as covers of magazines like *Space News* and *Aviation Week* that featured profiles on our clients.

"This is great, Janet," she exclaimed, sweeping her hand in front of her to note the office and the neat files of ongoing projects that lined my desk. "I am very impressed. Really. It's not easy starting a business and you did it! You should be so proud of yourself."

What a way to start a meeting! I couldn't help but smile at her approving words. Yes, it was an accomplishment. In all my feelings of guilt and failure, I sometimes forgot that running a business *was* challenging, and very few small businesses made it for very long, especially when faced with recession and disruptive events like the 9/11 terrorist attacks. "Thank you," I told her. "It is so nice to hear someone say that—especially since things have been a little rough of late."

"Yes, I can see that," she said, as she walked over and sat down across from me. She then reached into her briefcase and pulled out the file of papers I'd sent her.

Mom reappeared with two cups of coffee before disappearing again. I knew she would be in the next room praying.

"Now, given that you've hit this tough spot tell me: What have you done to try to turn things around?" Beth inquired.

Again, a first. No banker before now had ever asked me that. She didn't want to know how I felt about the business or what I wanted the bank to do for me or even how I had gotten myself into this mess. Nor did she start asking me to explain the financials—or worse, start trying to explain them to me. She wanted to know what I'd done to save my own business. In other words, what kind of skin did I have in the game? I think it was one of the wisest questions I'd ever been asked. It got right to the core: How willing was I to act? How committed was I to succeeding?

I went into presentation mode and began to tick off the many things I'd done to try to dig my way out of the pit:

"I've cut overhead by 60 percent."

"I haven't taken a salary since February."

"I took out most of the money in my 401(k)."

"I took a home equity loan out against my house."

"We quit having a local bank buy our invoices upfront."

"I have a finance and accounting expert helping me on a pro bono basis."

She listened intently, never once looking away or taking notes. I elaborated a bit more on our overall plan and told her how I'd been upfront with the clients about my financial situation, but they had chosen to stick it out with me. "I have really loyal clients who value what we do for them, and I feel like their businesses are beginning to rebound, which will bode well for us in the future."

I had covered everything, as far as I was concerned, so I stopped and waited for the next question. It never came.

"We're going to help you," she stated.

"I'm sorry, can you say that again?" Her words truly hadn't registered with me.

"We're going to help you—I'm going to make this happen."

"You are?!" I squeaked, my voice a few decibels higher than normal. I had taken John's advice. I had been confident. I had been focused. But the minute I heard Beth's response, my facade came tumbling down. "Really?! You're serious?"

"Yes," she smiled, clearly amused by my reaction. She knew how JANSON looked on paper, and it wasn't good, but she knew that didn't tell the whole story. She wanted to evaluate me from a relational point of view. My answers, she explained, had been honest and truthful and she could tell that I was willing to do just about anything to save my business.

"Yes, you've gotten yourself into a tough position," she acknowledged. "But you've done the hard part—you are working to help yourself get out of it."

She paused for a moment and took a sip of her coffee. "You see, most of the time when people come to the bank for money, they haven't made the tough adjustments. They want the bank to do all the work to dig them out of the mess. But you've already started the work. You've grabbed the shovel and you've started digging. That's impressive. I don't see that too often, and so I am going to find a way to get our bank to do this deal."

I could *not* believe it. We both began laughing, and I reached over and hugged her. "Thank you so much," I told her.

Not surprisingly, there was a catch. "You will need someone to co-sign for you," she cautioned. "You'll need someone to put up some collateral to go against the loan."

"Of course," I said. Jim and I knew this would be part of the deal. We were asking for a big loan, close to half a million dollars.

No bank in the world would give that on a simple signature.

Who would co-sign a loan that big? I didn't know, but I trusted that God did. I called out to my mother. She rushed in and then stopped when she saw both of us smiling broadly. She raised her eyes heavenward and clasped her hands together. I knew that she was thanking God. Soon, I was thanking Him too.

L ater that afternoon, I called Jim at home to tell him the good news. In his usual steadfast way, he didn't react much, but I knew he was pleased. He agreed that this was a positive breakthrough, but he also treated it as just more step forward on a long path. "We're heading in the right direction, I'll give you that," he told me. "You got any thoughts on how we're going to collateralize this?"

"Not really," I said.

My house was off the table. My retirement was pretty much gone. I had briefly entertained asking my mother to put up the equity in her house, which had been largely paid off, but quickly nixed the idea. I had already put my own home at risk; I didn't feel it was right to ask my mother also to risk her home. My family tree didn't have any big money branches on it. I'd asked Uncle Warren to help once, and he had been more than generous; Jim, on my direction, was already dipping into JANSON's limited funds to send my uncle $1800 a month until the loan was paid off.

There was a long silence between Jim and me. "I guess, I'm just going to pray about it," I said.

"Well, keep praying, but I think I might have a possibility," he said. "Have I ever told you about Billy?"

— TEN —

BREAKING OUT

...And the desert shall rejoice and blossom as the rose. It shall blossom abundantly and rejoice....They shall see the glory of the Lord, the excellency of our God. Isaiah 35:1-2

B illy? I dipped into my memories of the many phone conversations I'd had with Jim over the past couple of months and tried to recall him discussing anything remotely related to somebody with that name, but nothing matched.

"I know quite a few Billys," I replied. "But I don't think I know your Billy. What's his deal?"

Jim knew a lot of people. He was an administrator at an elite private school, so it wouldn't surprise me if he rubbed elbows with some big wigs around Atlanta who might easily have a half-million dollars in assets lying around doing nothing. Still, the name he'd dropped seemed a little informal for the typical CEO, venture capitalist or philanthropist.

"He goes to my church," Jim explained.

I nudged Jim for more details. "But who is he?"

Jim hesitated a bit, likely thinking we might be getting ahead of ourselves, but then he relented. Billy, it turned out, was quite a character and had quite the unexpected story. "He's just this good old country boy, and around here, everybody just assumes that he lives paycheck to paycheck," Jim said, explaining that he was a little scruffy around the edges.

Except when at church, Billy could usually be found in worn-out blue jeans and driving an older truck. He had worked for the same employer for 35 years and had never married. He was middle-aged and lived on the same farm as his parents. As Jim saw it, he was one of those semi-visible sorts, who didn't draw much attention, negative or positive, the type that most people tended to look past, sure there wasn't too much more to the character than what they saw on the outside.

"But they don't know Billy like I know Billy," Jim stated flatly. Despite being essentially footloose and fancy-free, Billy never spent his money foolishly. If he needed a new truck, he'd buy one that was ten years old and keep it running as long as he possibly could. He was frugal and resourceful. Jim admired that in Billy. "He can do just about anything with his hands: install wiring, lay concrete, build anything," Jim noted. "He's a real jack of all trades."

I was waiting, heart in my throat, to learn where this was all going. How exactly was Billy going to help us? Did he have a rich uncle who had died and left him everything? I had become slightly more patient when it came to waiting on God, but Jim's slow walk to the point of this story was killing me.

"And?" I prompted.

"And at some point, Billy asked me if I would take a look at his portfolio and give him some advice on what he should do with it."

Jim started to chuckle. "I'm thinking to myself at the time, 'He's probably got about $20,000.' Well, then I found out it wasn't $20,000. I was pretty amazed when I saw the whole portfolio. Let's just say it's enough that if somebody around here found out how well off he is, they might try to marry him."

Jim laughed again, but I was still trying to get my head around the meaning of this story. "And you say, now, he might be able to help me, that he might want to help me? I asked, incredulous. "Why?"

"Well, he knows I've been helping you on the side, and we've chit-chatted a little bit about it after church from time to time," Jim explained. "A few days ago, though, he came up to me and asked if there was anybody I knew that needs some help. He basically said, 'I just feel led that I'm to do something right now and help someone a little.'"

Jim cleared his throat before continuing. "Billy has given some money to the private Christian school where Jeannette and I teach, so I figured that's what he was talking about, so I said, 'Well, you know, I think we might have some more needs at the school.' But Billy came back with, 'No, I don't know if that's where I'm to give this time. I don't know if that's where the Lord is leading me.'"

I waited silently to hear what Jim would say next.

"So I told him that I was still working with you and that we were hoping you might get things lined up with a local bank after six rejections," Jim finally continued.

"What did he say?" I asked.

"He said he'd been wondering how you were doing," Jim said, adding that he had explained that we were hanging on, that we'd used a lot of my personal money to shore up the debt situation but that we still had a long way to go.

Someone from 700 miles away who I'd never met was wondering how I was doing. *This is unbelievable.*

Jim interrupted my thoughts. "I see Billy almost every Sunday. I'll let you know if he expresses any more interest in you and JANSON."

We were making progress—or at least it sure felt that way. For the first time in a while, things were happening, and we were inching our way up the mountainside. Beth at First Union Bank was willing to give JANSON a consolidation loan as soon as we had someone willing to co-sign and collateralize the loan. And Jim potentially had someone in mind. My confidence was beginning to soar. Whether it all came together now or at some later date with different players, I was even more convinced that God had a plan and He would deliver me from this financial morass I'd led my company into. In my heart, I knew it was just a matter of time.

Still, I was realistic. Even if the consolidation loan came through tomorrow, I still needed business to pick up. The ongoing work we had involved a series of small, minor projects, enough to pay the core bills but not enough to keep us going for very long—and certainly not enough to start me back on a salary.

Each day at JANSON, I devoted a good part of my time to new business development. I networked. I stayed up on market trends. I attended industry trade shows, working the floors, working the receptions, talking up our capabilities and handing my business card out to anyone who would take it. Still, it seemed that everyone in our markets was still in a bit of a holding pattern. No one was quite ready to invest in major new big-dollar projects.

Of course, I had options to bring in more money: For starters, I could reach out beyond my target market. A lot of local businesses needed one-off advertising and marketing help; back when we had started JANSON, Jeff and I had relied on medical practices and other small companies to bring in extra money and get us going while we worked to get a foot in the door at major space and aviation prospects. But now? No way. I'd spent too much time building up JANSON's brand as a high-quality marketing communications firm focused on these markets. I didn't want to take the easy way out, which could potentially water down our brand focus and reputation. More practically, choosing to do fill-in tasks for non-target clients could end up tying up my time to such a degree that I would be less available to my existing clients when their own workloads finally started to pick up significantly.

Mom constantly prayed for a breakthrough, and she remained upbeat. "We're just waiting for that right phone call," she would say, which I found mildly funny given how, not that long ago, the sound of debtors calling on that same phone had left us feeling overwhelmed and irritated.

Where JANSON was concerned, I had no choice but to wait for the market to turn. But going without a paycheck was getting more and more difficult. Austerity didn't come naturally to me, but for months now I had somehow managed to put a successful stranglehold on my personal spending. One week, I allotted myself just $5 for my food budget. I headed to the local grocery store and walked out with a large jar of generic peanut butter, a small jar of jelly and a loaf of white bread. That week, I ate sandwiches for breakfast and lunch—and headed over to my mother's house every night for dinner. Needless to say, the self-denial was starting to wear on me.

I was already working at least 60 hours each week at JANSON, but somehow I needed to find a way to bring in some extra income. I decided to get a part-time job. By working more evening hours at JANSON, I could free up my Saturdays and Sunday afternoons, so why not use them to bring in some spare change and ease the pressure on my budget? One Friday afternoon, I headed out to various golf courses in the region and filled out applications for whatever job happened to be open: driving the snack/beverage cart, serving as a marshal, even cleaning bathrooms. I was willing to do anything to ease the financial burden just a little bit.

By the end of the day, I'd submitted three applications. I drove to my mother's house for dinner and told her what I'd done.

"You're kidding!" she said.

"Nope," I replied, explaining that even a few hours of work would help with the groceries or the electric bill.

"Well, good on you, Jan, for doing whatever it takes to make it through all of this."

"I'm hoping they'll get back to me soon," I said. "I mean how many applications could they possibly get for cleaning bathrooms?"

I was back to waiting. On Monday morning, I must have traveled back and forth from my office to my mother's desk at least five times before noon. I was really eager to have some actual cash again floating around inside my wallet.

"Don't worry, Jan. Something will work out," my mother stated. "Just hang in there."

The offices were fairly silent the rest of the day and into Tuesday afternoon, but at 6 p.m., long after Mom had gone home, the phone rang. I was putting on my coat and getting ready to leave. I rushed over to my desk to grab the receiver, still standing when I breathlessly answered, "JANSON Communications."

"Janet Chihocky, please," I heard a voice say.

It wasn't one of the golf courses or even Jim. This was somebody new altogether. Was it a telemarketer? A creditor?

"This is she," I replied suspiciously, even as I maneuvered from the front of the desk around to the back so that I could sit down.

"Hi, this is Paula from DRS Technologies. We are looking for a company to handle our marketing and communications business."

I felt my legs go out from beneath me and I plopped down into my chair. *Whoa.* DRS wasn't an aerospace company but a major defense contractor. They were famous for having developed an anti-submarine detection system, but they also built a lot of other types of weapons and command systems.

I suddenly remembered chatting with a few of their sales guys at the trade show in Florida that I'd attended several months back.

One of them told me about the rocket ride of growth DRS had been on of late, relying on innovation and acquisitions to zip from $58 million in revenue in 1994 to more than $500 million by 2002. "We think we're probably going to reach a billion within the next two or three years," he had said. I was impressed. I gave both of them my business card, one of the hundreds I would give out over the next several months, but I didn't think anything more of it. DRS was pure defense, not aerospace. Why would they be calling me?

I pulled the chair closer to the desk and guardedly answered in my most professional tone. "Can you tell me a little bit about what you're looking for?" I answered. Don't act too eager, I thought. Maybe she just wanted a reference.

"We need a firm right away to help us with a new campaign," she said. "One of our salespeople gave me your card, and I'd like you to come to New Jersey and meet with me."

I could feel my hand start to shake, forcing me to tighten the grip I had on the receiver. *Oh Lord, this is it.* "Yes, of course. When would you like to meet?" I asked matter-of-factly.

"As soon as possible. Can you fly up the day after tomorrow?"

This time, I nearly dropped the phone, but I managed to compose myself long enough to write down all the details. This was a potential game changer. Not only would it be a lot of immediate work, but it would also be a foothold in a new, equally lucrative market. Our clients sometimes sold satellites and space technology to defense and military agencies, but DRS lived completely in that world.

After hanging up, I called my mother. "You will not believe the phone call I just got," I said, not stopping long enough to give her a chance to guess. She knew it was good news, but I spoke so fast, she had to stop me in the middle to ask me to repeat everything more slowly.

She let out a big breath when I finally finished. "Oh, praise the

Lord," she said. "Jan, He *never* fails. See, you just needed to hang in there."

When Melinda heard, she rushed over to my house, carrying an exquisite St. John suit from her collection. It was coal black and gorgeous, and she was loaning it to me for the next day's presentation. "If you want to make a million bucks, you've got to dress like you can handle a million bucks," she grinned, as she handed the outfit to me. "So wear it like you own it."

I did as she said. The suit fit perfectly, and when I walked into the lobby at DRS headquarters, I looked and acted like the total executive package. One guy standing off to the side noticed me and declared, "Wow, you're wearing St. John. Very nice."

"Thank you," I replied evenly, as if I heard this sort of thing all the time. "That's very kind of you."

Drawing once again on the advice that my client John had given me before my bank meeting, I walked into the conference room with focus and a self-assured smile, reaching out immediately to shake Paula's hand. "It's so nice to finally meet you," I said. I was desperate for the account, but I could not—and would not—act desperate. This company needed a new firm to develop ad campaigns for a number of recently developed products, along with the associated marketing collateral, like product brochures, sell sheets, case studies and web pages. It was big, and I took my time to highlight why JANSON's strengths and capabilities would dovetail with their specific needs and then answered their many questions concisely and authoritatively. Before the day was done, they let me know that they wanted JANSON to take over the account.

When I told Jim, he shared my excitement, but he also took a moment to caution me against losing discipline. No matter how big the workload got, we still needed a consolidation loan. This account would help us to break even in our day-to-day operations and perhaps begin to give us a bit of breathing room. However, by itself, the work wouldn't make any real dent in the debt load. "And don't even think about going all loose with any spending," he ordered gruffly. "Nothing's changed. We need to keep going, business as usual, or you'll be back in the same boat."

By Jim's order, JANSON's cash flow would continue to be managed with the same level of order, precision and discipline as anything he ever oversaw in the Air Force.

"I totally get it and I'm with you on this," I replied. And so for the time being, there would be no reprieve for me. My salary would remain as it had been for months—a big, fat nothing. I would continue to limit my spending to little more than my most basic needs. And my stable of consultants and I would do all of this work as JANSON was in no position as yet to hire even a single full-time employee. Still, the new account proved to be a rainstorm of blessings. JANSON was once again humming with creativity.

All we needed now was a co-signer for the consolidation loan. Jim was still waiting to hear back from Billy, and there was a part of me that yearned to take charge and try to find one on my own. But I didn't. My journey through the valley thus far had made me sure of one thing: God would work it all out in His time, and I needed to wait to see it unfold.

One Sunday afternoon, about a week later, Jim called. He rarely contacted me on the weekend, and I could tell by the tone of his voice that he had something important to say. At that moment, I thought I would burst, so I came right out and asked, "Did you talk to Billy?"

"Yeah, I did," he said. As usual, Jim's voice was flat and devoid of much emotion, disguising any sense of whether this was going to be good news or bad.

"Okay," I said. I took a gulp of air and prayed quickly: *Your will, God, not mine.*

"I told him that we had a bank that was definitely willing to work with you, but we needed a co-signer for a loan of a half-million dollars," Jim said.

He took a moment to clear his throat before continuing. "He's going to pray about it, and I'll probably see him next week."

I was speechless, a definite rarity for me. Could this really be a possibility? I prayed all week, and so did everyone else in my inner circle. That someone who had never met me—someone who knew very little about me or my business—was actually thinking about helping me was a miracle in and of itself. I wanted to pray: *Let it be as I want it, Lord,* but I realized that it had been my direction and my steering that had taken JANSON off course and into a ditch. So, I prayed as I should: *Your will, Lord, not mine.* And I prayed it over and over again.

The following Sunday afternoon, I waited as long as I could before I picked up the phone and called Jim. "What did Billy say?" I asked eagerly as soon as I heard his voice.

Jim seemed confused for a moment. "Oh, right, Billy," he replied casually. "Yeah, he couldn't make it to church today, so maybe I'll see him next week."

So calm. So nonchalant. As if we had all the time in the world. I had waited all week in anticipation. I was so eager for an answer—one way or the other—and now nothing. I really thought I might burst wide open at this moment. And then I realized that I was once again ignoring God's call for me to be patient. I had taken a step forward this week in that effort and now I had just taken two steps back. *Forgive me, God,* I prayed silently. *I'll keep trying.* I knew He knew that I was a work in progress.

"Hey, Janet, I'll let you know as soon as I know more," Jim

said, shutting down any opening for conversation. "You have a great rest of your weekend."

And so I went back to work on Monday and back to working hard to keep my focus on the here and now. Each morning, I did my devotions and prayed: *Fill my cup, Lord, with exactly what I need for today.* By the end of the week, I was at peace. No matter what happened, God was with me and He would work it all for good.

The following Sunday, I had just gotten home from church when Jim called. "I saw Billy today," he announced. "He prayed about it and he feels led to help you."

I was so elated that I didn't even know how to respond except: "What did you just say?"

Jim repeated the statement, but then his voice seemed to take on a lower, more ominous tone. "I had to be honest with him, Janet. I had to set the expectation, so he really understood what's going on with JANSON. So I told him, 'There's a 50 percent chance that she'll make it and a 50 percent chance that she's not going to make it.'"

I felt the excitement I'd built up slowly start to seep out like a shrinking balloon. This information would surely have muted his interest. I was no sure bet. In fact, I was a gamble, a long shot. Why would anyone take a chance on me after hearing those odds?

"So, what did he say?" I whispered apprehensively, no longer certain I wanted to know the answer.

I heard Jim take a deep breath and blow it back out audibly. "He said, 'You know, Jim, I hear you, but what I have is God's money, and if He wants it back He can have it. I can't explain it. All I know is that God has told me to help this woman.'"

I felt a chill run through me, and once again, I didn't know how to respond. Somebody I'd never met, who lived 700 miles away, was going to help me by putting up half a million dollars worth of collateral. Why? Because God had told him to. I suddenly remembered that first night on this journey when God had led me to keep going with JANSON—against all the odds. I had surrendered to His will. And as promised, God had opened every single door that needed an opening at just the right time.

"Are you serious?" I asked.

"Yes," he replied flatly.

"Really? Truly? I tried to keep my voice low, but I was losing the fight. "I cannot believe this!" I finally yelled.

I heard Jim laughing at my outburst. I could tell that he was just as amazed at this turn of events as I was, but as usual, he managed to stay in total control. I pulled myself together and tried to think and act like an executive.

"Okay, great," I said, getting my emotions under control and putting on my professional demeanor. "Let's talk next steps: I guess I'll put together a business plan for him and send him some samples of our work and a copy of my resumé. Then I guess I could come down after that and meet with him so that we can go over the details of the arrangement. I'm sure he has a lot of questions he'll need to be answered. I guess we need to get a lawyer involved."

I was all over the map with my thoughts. I started feeling around my kitchen for a pen and a pad of paper.

"No," Jim answered.

I stopped looking. "No what?" I asked, confused. "No to which part?"

"All of it," Jim insisted. "No, he doesn't need a business plan. No, he didn't ask for a meeting. No, he doesn't want to see your resumé. No, we don't need a lawyer."

"Does he want to at least speak with me on the phone?"

"Nope. But I think you should send him some of your marketing brochures because he's not exactly sure what it is that you do."

Was this some kind of joke? "Jim—really, you're not serious,"

I stated. "Who does this?"

If the roles were reversed, I would have been demanding meetings, a business plan, a deed to somebody's house, my name in the will. Half a million dollars was a lot of money—in Billy's case, it was a big percentage of everything he'd worked for his whole life.

"I mean, come on, who does this?" I repeated. My question was meant to be hypothetical because I knew there was no real answer to it. Jim and I both recognized that we had stumbled across a rare person of pure faith, the type you assumed could only be found in the Bible or in books recounting the history of the saints. I was awestruck. I had chosen to surrender to God and give Him free rein with JANSON's future and my own, but I had resisted the hard work at times, I had doubted, I had whined, I had nearly given up—and I had everything to gain.

But Billy? He had everything to lose and yet he'd surrendered mind, body and soul—no questions asked. It was a level of obedience and conviction that I could only aspire to.

"Well, Billy trusts me, I guess, but he really trusts God, so go ahead and tell the banker to draw up the papers."

I shouldn't have been surprised. God had told me that He would deliver me—in His way, in His time. Still, I couldn't help myself. It was too much. I stood straight up and raised my hands—and the phone receiver—high in the air.

"Unbelievable!" I shouted.

I called my mom first. "You are not going to believe this!" I told her. How many times had I asked her that on this journey? Too many to count.

She answered in her usual way. "God always answers prayers."

We both laughed, and she insisted on being in the office the next morning when I called First Union. I pushed the button for the speakerphone. "Beth, guess what?" I teased. "I've got a co-signer."

"What? You're kidding?"

I told her the details, and she listened quietly, not saying anything for a long while after I finished. I could only imagine how it must have bowled her over. "Well, Janet, I have to say: This is a first for me," she finally replied. "Congratulations! I am so thrilled for you."

Within three days, she had the paperwork drawn up. She sent it to me for review, and I sent it on to Jim. By the following Tuesday, Jim had FedExed everything back to me. I reached in and pulled out the documents. On one page was Billy's signature collateralizing the loan. Another page contained details about the assets that guaranteed the loan. It was done.

I personally took the papers to First Union, and within a few days, we had a loan for $500,000. I called Jim to let him know that the funds were now available and he could start to do his magic with the rest of the debt. I was over the moon and I could tell that Jim was too.

Little by little, Jim tapped into the loan as he began negotiating payoffs with creditors. In September, I started drawing a small salary again, and JANSON also started paying Jim a monthly retainer. Work with our new defense account kept us very busy, and our existing clients had picked up significantly as well. We were so busy that I was actually beginning to think about hiring a couple of full-time employees. By late November, Jim had finished negotiations, and we'd paid off all the debtors using the First Union funds.

Now we had seven years to pay off the loan and release Billy's collateral, a timeframe longer than JANSON had even been in business. Could we do it?

—ELEVEN—

UNEXPECTED DELIVERANCE

Jesus said to her, "Did I not say to you that if you would believe you would see the glory of God?" John 11:40

JANSON did, in fact, "make" it. We came face to face with Chapter 11, but I never filed for bankruptcy. And while we had seven years to pay off the half-million dollar debt consolidation loan, we would, in just over two years, pay down enough of it to fully release Billy's collateral and his co-signer commitment.

Fast forward to 2020. As I write this book, JANSON is in its 22nd year of operation and is a thriving multimillion-dollar small business. It is profitable, diverse, debt-free and making an impact for our clients.

My story isn't only a story of one person's business turnaround and success, however. I tell people all the time that I am just a player in a larger story that was all about God. It is really a story of surrender, deliverance and listening to God's voice, even when the facts seem to state otherwise. It's a story of what happens when you trust God to lead you in your trials, to carry you when you don't have enough strength to keep going and to bring all the right, often unlikely, resources that you need to make it through.

How else could anyone explain Billy? I think of him often, and his "silent testimony," as I like to call it, remains an inspiration to me. I pray it will also be an inspiration for everyone reading this book. Billy's willing heart—"What I have is God's money, and if He wants it back, then He can have it"—demonstrates exactly what the faith talk and walk is supposed to look like: total trust, total obedience, total surrender.

He was not acting as an anonymous donor making a pledge. Rather, this was an individual who acted on what he was led to do—with no preconditions, no prerequisites, no strings attached. He completely and unequivocally trusted the Lord. Talk about obedience! To this day, I have never met Billy nor spoken to him on the phone. (I have reached out several times through the years, but he has preferred to stay in the background and I have respected that.)

The impact of what Billy did and his willingness to obey God's call to help a stranger cannot be overstated, both in terms of what it meant to me personally and what it meant to the survival and rebirth of JANSON.

As I've already shared, I could see God's hand in everything: every trial, every challenge, every breakthrough, every penny, every dollar. "When you go through the waters, I will be with you" is what He tells us in Isaiah 43:2. I don't believe it is possible to look at all of these twists, turns and unbelievable events in my story and see anything other than: "Look at what God did!" In fact, one of the key players in JANSON's turnaround couldn't help but marvel at all that had happened in my struggle and chose, shortly after that, to accept Christ and become a committed believer.

Looking back on God's unexpected deliverance, I realize now that failing moments or collapsing seasons in our lives are not just about somehow getting to the other side of the bridge; they're also about becoming better, stronger, more open to change, more understanding and more accepting of the Holy Spirit's work in and through our lives. Job 23:10 says, "But He knows the way that I take: When He has tested me, I shall come forth as gold."

I would love to tell you that in the immediate aftermath of this experience, I somehow "arrived" as the model Christian businesswoman. I did not.

There were times when, in the daily pressures and new challenges of business, I would find myself retreating back to a lot of the same unhealthy behaviors that I had been dealing with leading up to and during the year in which I nearly lost everything. These included management styles and controlling behaviors that were learned behaviors deeply rooted in my life experience and psyche and that I needed to desperately unlearn. I didn't know how.

Changing and growing is crazy hard work—and it's uncomfortable. But I've learned the hard way that God is more interested in my character than He is in my comfort.

And so I spent time working on myself. Several years ago, I hired a business coach to provide a lot of the "executive" training I'd missed in my rush to become a businesswoman, and I still seek her counsel to this day. I took a good hard look at my life and the mistakes that I'd made, came to terms with them and found reasons to be grateful. Today, I am even thankful for the lesson in accountability that my mother—and yes, my school too—provided as a result of my actions with the Red Plastic Cup. If we wait for life's lessons to be fair, we'll be waiting a long time! I've learned that it's more about owning my responsibility and not running when the going gets tough.

For me, the issue of forgiveness has been another important lesson. For a long time after my year of facing bankruptcy, I couldn't quite let go of the hurt and anger I felt towards the employees who had quit and then tried to steal my clients— despite the fact that they failed in their attempt and that I never saw or spoke with them again after confronting them at the Florida trade show in early 2002.

Fourteen years later, though, as I was driving to a meeting, I got a phone call out of the blue from one of those employees. "I am so sorry," I heard him say, almost as soon as I answered. "I have felt so guilty all this time for what I did. I've tried to move beyond it, but I just couldn't because I knew I owed you an apology."

I could hear the sincerity in his voice, and I promptly let go of the feelings I'd clung to for so long. "Thank you," I replied softly. "It's great to hear from you."

The timing couldn't have been more perfect. While it took that individual 14 years to give his apology, it had also taken me 14 years to accept that apology and forgive him unconditionally. I am convinced that during all that time, through a variety of trials, challenges and grace, God was working on my heart, softening it and infusing it with compassion for others.

As I worked through all this, I realized that I had a new mindset, and that led to new desires for my business and my own sense of purpose. I wanted the company to be more valuable to our clients, of course, but interestingly, as time went on, I felt led to work with a brand-new type of client: the U.S. military.

At the time, our young men and women were fighting terrorism on the front lines in hotspots around the world, and I felt like I was meant to do my own part by helping military branches tell their story and communicate their value. To go from representing commercial aerospace and defense companies to being a direct-to-government defense contractor for the military, led by a female who had never served in the military, never worn the uniform—well, that seemed like one tall order!

So I embarked on trying to climb yet another massive and quite intimidating mountain. By relying on the Lord to lead my steps and building on all the lessons I'd learned during my time in the valley, my employees and I pushed ahead with everything we had. But where would we even start to begin making this monstrous transition into the military, an extremely unique, complex and tightly knit market? Where would we find a breakthrough or a glimmer of hope that we could do it?

It wasn't easy. I can tell you that I spent years investing in learning about this new market. I talked to military officers who were willing to mentor me. I worked non-stop researching, networking and writing proposals. I persevered when doors seemed to be constantly slamming in my face, shaking it off and writing more proposals—always with a focus on showing how JANSON could exceed requirements. And I prayed.

But then came a gorgeous Thursday afternoon in June 2007 that I'll never forget. I was sitting at my desk and suddenly my cell phone rang. It wasn't a number I recognized. Of course, it wasn't a creditor—we were long past those years—and it wasn't a client either. Curious, I picked up the phone and answered brightly: "Hi, this is Janet Chihocky."

The individual on the other end of the line introduced herself: "Hi Janet, this is Patty and I work on a program supporting the United States Army. Would you have a few minutes to talk? Your company came highly recommended to us."

And just like that, we were on our way to playing in a whole new, highly significant market. It had seemed a crazy ambition at first—but as I've seen over and over: No order is too tall when God is on your side. But that story is another book!

G etting back on your feet is never an easy feat, but as my story shows, it is not only possible, but it can lead you to places you could never imagine on your own. And remember: You'll always learn more lessons from falling down and getting back up than you will from those successful moments or the immediate bailout. So find ways to be grateful for the trials and enjoy the journey as best you can. It will make it a lot easier.

The journey I have taken—and indeed it has been quite a journey!—has taught me so many lessons that I couldn't possibly list them all. However, here are three takeaways that anyone can apply during both business and personal trials:

If you're not growing, you're dying.

We all need to grow in order to survive—people, businesses, even brands. And yes, growth is hard. It's humbling. It's uncomfortable. It's painful. But it's absolutely necessary. I had a lot of growing up to do during my Chapter 11 season, and to do that, my journey had to be about a lot more than just getting out of debt. I needed to listen to strong counsel who didn't sugarcoat it. I needed to grow up and accept my responsibility. This is not the time to seek out "yes" people who tell you what you want to hear! No, find those people who care about you, who believe in you, but who will also tell it to you straight. For me, Jim, of course, was the man for this job. He provided me with very direct, very candid, critical feedback, and it was, at times, hard to take. The reality, though, is that if I wanted to get out of this mess that I was responsible for, I needed to not just survive it—I needed to grow from it, to learn from it. Being the impatient person that I am, you've got to know that I was itching to get out of this hot mess, right here, right now!

But Jim and others helped me realize pretty early on that if I wasn't willing to change—change how I did things with the company but also change *me*—not only was I unlikely to make it through, but I was going to be right back in a similar mess pretty quick. Only, maybe this time, instead of a business or financial issue, it might affect something in my personal life, something that might actually be harder to bounce back from.

So getting back on your feet after you've been knocked down will require you to identify and find ways to change those "learned behaviors" and habits that played a role in putting you on the ground in the first place. When you're faced with a trial, don't just rush to pass "Go," grab your $200 and act like everything's normal. You'll lose eventually.

Instead, take the time to really assess yourself and learn from this season. I believe that Chapter 11 moments, as I like to call them, can hold powerful promises for every one of us. Pray intensely and ask God to reveal these issues and behaviors that may be holding you back and to give you the strength to help you overcome and retire those destructive traits. Lean on friends and family who believe in you, but again, don't give in to the temptation of surrounding yourself with "yes" people who don't have the wisdom or courage to tell you what you need to hear. If necessary, seek out a mentor or work with a therapist.

Can you do it? Yes, because with Christ, anything is possible! He has unlimited power and resources—but you have to call on Him. Is being down and out for a season easy? Absolutely not. But it can be a real blessing, an opportunity for growth that will take you farther than would have otherwise been possible. Don't be afraid to grow, and get comfortable with being uncomfortable.

Aim at nothing and you'll reach it every time.

I heard this piece of advice years ago and it's stuck with me ever since. No matter what you're doing in life, you have got to set targets and put together a plan for reaching them. A lot of people avoid goals out of fear—usually fear of failure. Of course, nobody wants to fail, but one reason that people do fail is that they usually set the bar too high.

Goal-setting is a great activity for me and the one thing I've learned is that goals have to be realistic if they are going to be achievable. Everyone knows the dieter who makes a plan to eat 1,000 calories a day and lose 50 pounds in two months. For all their trouble, most of them don't reach their goal—and a lot of them end up actually *gaining* weight!

Here's my point: Setting a target gives you a visual to get and keep you on track. The target should be challenging but not so hard that you end up either 1) completely burning yourself out, along with everyone around you, or 2) getting frustrated and calling it quits. I've seen companies set unrealistic business targets—I mean, totally *insane* targets. One business I know expected its employees to achieve a 30 percent market share in a new region with low-brand visibility in just 36 months. Not only could the workers themselves not see it happening, but the expensive market research data the company paid for didn't support the idea that it was even close to being doable. Still, the company went full-court press. What happened? They never attained the 30 percent market share, and they had to finally pull back the reins. And for what? All they ended up getting was a lot of defeated, demoralized employees.

Those are the kinds of targets that should be avoided, the "Hey, let's get caught up in big numbers and push everything we've got as hard as we can" targets. Always remember: The *Titanic* was on a steady track to arrive in New York on time and still upright until Bruce Ismay, the ship's financier and builder, pressured the captain to speed up, in hopes of undercutting the target and generating headlines. He got headlines alright—just not the ones he wanted!

So be careful about pushing targets beyond what is reasonable, but, at the same time, don't shy away from setting realistic targets. Visualize yourself on the other side of your Chapter 11 moment. Visualize yourself making more money. Visualize yourself debt-free. Visualize restored relationships.

Many don't share my views on this, and that's fine. But what has worked successfully for me both personally and professionally is to aim at a target that will stretch me but not kill me, stretch my company but not overly burden my employees in the process. As a result, our growth has remained slow but steady over the years. There's a lot to be said for that.

Where you are today is not nearly as important as the direction you're headed.

Direction is the operative word here. A lot of people may be driving fast to get out of their situation, but they're headed south instead of north. So what's the lesson? It's not how quickly you can recover or rebound, but rather to first make sure that you're headed in the right direction. That's going to be key to any successful recovery.

Golf is a good metaphor for this. I love the game, but anyone who's ever been out to a golf course knows that new golfers are all about trying to deliver a power drive—as high and as far as possible. Whoosh...there it goes! But in what direction? I see guys all the time at the driving range, giving that swing everything they've got. A few of them get the intended result: a nice, long drive straight down the fairway. In other words, in the right direction. Most, however, are just gripping, grunting and swinging as hard as they can, and they are getting distance...but where is that ball headed? Tree-bound, at best, but more likely *out* of bounds in a sandtrap or in a lake. Talk about frustration!

These golfers want instant gratification and, as a result, are not willing to take the time or the steps necessary to make sure the ball is at least headed in the right direction. To stay on course, you need focus—and patience.

This applies to every aspect of life. Where do you need to be? Set your course and then don't stray. Focus is critical—not just for going in the right direction but also staying there. Watch carefully for roadblocks and hurdles that will push you off track. Maybe there are friends and relationships or bad habits that inhibit your ability to stay focused on your new direction. Trust me, I have had to walk away from certain environments and acquaintances because they disrupted my focus. They might be good people, but they were not headed in the same direction I was headed. There are business partners that JANSON opted not to work with any longer when they began to impede our chosen path.

So remain focused on the course that yields you a positive outcome, on a horizon that puts you and your family in a good place, on a place that is healthy and where you know that God desires you to be. That is when we know the direction is right—when it aligns with His plans and His desires for our lives. I have made many directional choices that I thought were great at the time, but they were not aligned with God's plan.

When working on getting out of a bad situation, our first instinct is to act, to do something, anything. Trust me, I know because I have been been guilty of this response and paid a heavy price. So no matter how frustrated and impatient you feel, try to resist this temptation. Don't just grab the first solution you see. If you're in a financial crunch, it will be tempting to deposit that cash advance the credit card company is offering you or accept the first job available.

Don't give in to this kind of pressure. Instead, take time to catch your breath, even if it's only for 15 minutes. This will allow you to gain perspective, to get your bearings. Where do you need to be? The answer won't always be evident. There are moments when you might take a tactical pause for an extended period to reassess your direction and then there are days when you might need to take a quick walk around the building and go to God in prayer for an answer to a pending issue.

In my case, I learned of my financial crisis on a Friday, which forced me to take the weekend, pause, gain some perspective and pray. As a result, I was able to get my emotions under control and then, with God's guidance and the support of friends and family, make a decision. It wasn't a lot of time, but it made all the difference in where I ended up.

I can tell you with certainty that the more time I have invested in His word over the past few years, the greater my ability to "hear" His voice more clearly. Pray for discernment. Ask Him to show you His plans for you. And that's because, in the end, any kind of adversity in life is about placement. Where are you meant to be so that your potential is maximized? What is the direction you should be heading to achieve the outcome you were created for?

Finally, this concept of traveling in the right direction is something that can apply in many areas of life. There is personal direction, financial direction, business direction. Nothing, however, matters more than your eternal direction. To borrow a statement from evangelist Anne Graham Lotz: "I've lived long enough to know that Jesus is real." Quite simply, I know without a doubt that I would not be where I am today without Jesus Christ.

In writing this book, my hope is that everyone reading it will also see that God is real, that He works in our lives and that He desires to have a personal relationship with each one of us.

I'd be remiss if I didn't at least ask you to ask yourself: What is my eternal direction? Am I heading the right way? Do I know for sure that if I were to die tonight, I'm going to spend eternity in Heaven?

If you're not sure, I encourage you to read and follow this very simple plan of salvation that Jesus Himself provided to us.

1) Admit that you're a sinner in need of a Savior.
2) Believe that Jesus is Lord.
3) Call upon His name by asking Him into your heart and making Him the Lord and Savior of your life.

As the Apostle Paul explains in Romans 6:23: "For the wages of sin is death, but the gift of God is eternal life through Jesus Christ our Lord."

This is great news! Christ has done the work of the Cross and offers His grace as a gift. All you have to do is accept it.

Once you become a Christian, you always are one. Nothing can separate us from the love of God, as Paul also pointed out in Romans. However, walking the Christian walk is a lifelong pursuit, an opportunity to get to know God, to grow in your faith and to learn to be more like Christ. But the world—and our own sinful natures—can still get in the way and it's easy to get tempted, distracted, complacent and off course. When it does, you must once again stop, take stock and ask again: Where does God want me to be, and how do I get there?

This need to rethink my own direction has been a big focus and blessing for me over the past year. It all began when I had the opportunity to take a trip to Israel. Every person I know who has taken this pilgrimage to the Holy Land has raved about it. In fact, they couldn't come up with enough superlatives to describe the impact that "walking where Jesus walked" had on them.

For me, it was the perfect time to retreat from my professional life because my walk with Christ needed a refresh, a reset, a chance to go deeper. How better to do that than to follow in Jesus's own footsteps! As I began packing and making plans, though, I soon realized that I was not going to be in control of the itinerary. God was. I could feel Him prodding me, leading me, guiding my steps—so much so that by the time this trip was over, my faith, my outlook, my life and my purpose had been quietly but completely transformed.

Now I'm not saying that you have to go to Israel to reconnect with the Lord or have a transformational experience, any more than I would say that a fellow business owner has to go through a near-bankruptcy to put their company on better financial and operational footing.

What I *am* saying is that God has a plan for everyone and He works according to His own script and His own schedule. In my case, Israel happened to be the setting where God could get my full attention. His placement for you might be completely different. He might put you into a new job nine states away or He might send you across the street to help a neighbor in need.

The key is to listen for His direction, discern His will and then follow the plan. You'll be amazed to find that His agenda looks nothing like what you would put together.

Consider my trip to Israel. From the moment I landed in Tel Aviv, I started feeling like the Lord was providing me with some pretty unique instructions.

For one, I felt like I was not supposed to follow the crowds. Everyone who had taken this trip had recommended that I sign up for a guided, organized Biblical tour of Israel. This would take all the guesswork out of my schedule and ensure my safety. That, however, is not what I was led to do, which freed me to go at my own pace and pick and choose the places that I wanted to experience. These places included Jerusalem Old City, the Western Wall, the Israel Museum, the Mount of Olives, Masada, the Dead Sea, the Garden Tomb, the Church of the Holy Sepulchre and Via Dolorosa, or the "way of suffering" that Jesus traveled on His way to His crucifixion.

I also went to a popular place on the Jordan River where most Christian pilgrims renew their baptismal promises and new Christian converts are baptized. It's a modern site on the southern end of the Sea of Galilee that is maintained by a kibbutz. Of course, I believed that I should be baptized in the Jordan as a symbol of my renewed commitment to Christ, and so I had stuffed my bathing suit into my carry bag. But as I watched so many people in white robes wade into the river and allow themselves to be dipped backwards for total immersion in the Jordan's mild, clean waters, I balked. I was not feeling any desire nor, frankly, any leading that I was to do this. Didn't God want me to get baptized in this holy place? Why couldn't I make myself step into the line? Confused, I left and went on to my next destination.

Why *didn't* I want to get in the water? I asked myself over and over. What was wrong with me? Later, during my evening prayers, I asked God directly: "Isn't this what You wanted me to do?"

The feeling that I was supposed to get baptized still clung to me, and I couldn't shake it. I must be letting God down, I thought. I felt like a total hypocrite.

Three days later, I hopped in a car along with a fellow traveler for a visit to the Dead Sea. I again took my bathing suit along, just in case I had the opportunity to "float" in this ancient body of thick saltwater. But at one point, our driver suggested that since we had a little extra time, we should check out a lesser-known site that just happened to be nearby. "This is the original Jordan River where it is believed that John the Baptist baptized Jesus," he explained.

That got my attention. "Lead the way," I directed. When we got there, though, I quickly put away any notions I might have had about getting baptized in this place. This part of the river wasn't clean like the other site. It was *dirty*! Muddy and murky. Even from a distance, I could see large flying insects buzzing and hovering over the water. I could only imagine what lurked beneath. How disgusting! I thought, before turning to my fellow traveler and declaring out loud: "You could not *pay* me to get in this river." My suburban sensibilities shuddered at even the thought of it.

Still, Jesus had been here, so I started walking towards the water's edge. I planned to grab a quick photo and head right back out as fast as possible. But the closer I got to the river, the more I felt a strange pull on my spirit. I turned my head and noticed a pastor and a small group of people about 40 feet away. They were praying earnestly and lining up to be dunked in the grimy water. The scene was similar to the baptisms I'd seen at the other site, but this one seemed different, more intense, more powerful. Something was happening, something transcendent. I can't explain it, but the activity drew me in.

Slowly, I started making my way towards them and before long, I was standing alongside the river. Up close, the water looked even more filthy and I had no intention of getting wet. But I felt like God wanted me to observe and so I stood there, totally surrendered, totally obedient. After a while, I began to walk back up the stairs. I'm good, I thought. Then, I heard a voice: "Janet, this is where you are to be baptized."

No way, I thought. I am *not* getting in that river! I kept my eyes forward, moving up the steps quickly. If I kept my focus, I thought, I could escape without anyone noticing. But as I came to the top, I realized that I was running...running from the blessing, the double blessing, that God had for me in this place. I needed to obey. I needed to surrender.

Well, I turned and flew back down those steps! The pastor had just finished his final baptism when I rushed up to him. "I'm not traveling with a group or a pastor, but I am a born-again believer and I need to be baptized," I told him breathlessly. "Would you please baptize me?"

"I need to leave," he explained, but then he relented. "Go change—quickly."

I raced back up the steps, put on my bathing suit and raced back down again. Let me just say that I am not a runner, but people stopped and stared, and someone later told me that everyone was amazed at how fast I was moving.

As I reached the river's edge, I grabbed the hand of the gentleman helping the pastor, and the very *moment* my foot touched that water, it was as if the mud and the mire magically turned clear and pristine. To me, it looked and felt like holy water. The pastor began to pray and prophesy over me as if he'd known me my whole life. I can't even adequately describe the prayer, but I just knew that the Holy Spirit was speaking through him into my life. I released everything I'd been holding onto for years and surrendered fully as I was tipped backward into the murky waters, waters that provided a new life and a refreshed direction for me.

Afterward, the gentleman who had been helping the pastor came up and introduced himself. He was an accountant, he told me. "I fell on hard times once and thought I was going to have to file for bankruptcy, but God told me not to," he explained.

"No kidding!" I responded with a smile. "Well, let me tell you *my* story."

CHAPTER 11